Transportation Management
Strategies, Operations, and Innovations

CHAPTER 15: CONCLUSION AND BEST PRACTICES FOR EFFECTIVE TRANSPORTATION MANAGEMENT

Chapter 1: Introduction to Transportation Management

Transportation management is a cornerstone of the supply chain, ensuring that goods move efficiently from one point to another to meet consumer demand. This chapter introduces transportation management by discussing its role, significance in supply chains, primary objectives, and the different modes of transportation available.

1.1 Overview of Transportation Management

Transportation management encompasses the planning, execution, and optimization of the physical movement of goods. It is the backbone of logistics, involving a network of interconnected activities that include managing carriers, selecting routes, scheduling shipments, and tracking the movement of products to final destinations. Transportation management's main objective is to create an efficient and reliable flow of goods, balancing cost, speed, and reliability to satisfy customer needs.

Effective transportation management requires coordination between multiple stakeholders, including manufacturers, suppliers, carriers, and retailers. Given the complexity of modern supply chains, transportation management relies heavily on advanced technologies like Transportation Management Systems (TMS) that provide tools to manage, analyze, and optimize these logistical processes. TMS platforms offer insights into costs, routing, inventory levels, and delivery times, which support informed decision-making.

Transportation management also extends to monitoring key performance indicators (KPIs) such as on-time delivery rates, freight costs, and order accuracy. These metrics help logistics professionals assess how well the transportation function supports organizational objectives, ensuring goods arrive at the right place, time, and cost. In this way, transportation management enables companies to build resilience and agility into their supply chains, responding quickly to disruptions like demand fluctuations or route changes.

1.2 Importance in the Supply Chain

Transportation management is integral to a well-functioning supply chain. With efficient transportation, businesses can meet customer expectations, control costs, and maintain competitiveness in a global market. Below are key reasons why transportation management is vital in the supply chain:

1.2.1 Facilitating Product Flow and Timely Delivery

Transportation ensures the continuous movement of goods from suppliers to production facilities, then from facilities to warehouses, and finally to end customers. Delays in transportation disrupt this flow, leading to stockouts, lost sales, and customer dissatisfaction. By effectively managing transportation, companies maintain steady product flow and ensure goods arrive on schedule, ultimately strengthening customer relationships.

1.2.2 Cost Control and Budgeting

Transportation costs, including fuel, labor, and maintenance, form a significant portion of total supply chain expenses. Optimizing transportation can yield substantial cost savings. Transportation management involves selecting efficient routes, consolidating shipments, and negotiating favorable terms with carriers to control expenses. Companies also leverage technologies to optimize fuel usage and minimize costs, ensuring they stay within budget while providing timely deliveries.

1.2.3 Enhancing Supply Chain Resilience

A resilient supply chain can withstand disruptions, such as natural disasters or geopolitical tensions. Effective transportation management includes contingency planning, enabling companies to reroute shipments, use alternative modes, or collaborate with multiple carriers when unexpected issues arise. By anticipating and preparing for risks, businesses can maintain service levels and meet demand even during disruptions.

1.2.4 Supporting Global Supply Chains

Transportation management is essential for global supply chains, where goods are sourced and sold internationally. Cross-border logistics introduces complexities, such as customs regulations, tariffs, and varied carrier networks. Companies rely on transportation management to navigate these challenges, ensuring goods move smoothly across borders and minimizing delays and additional costs.

1.2.5 Customer Satisfaction and Competitive Advantage

Fast, reliable delivery services enhance customer satisfaction, which is critical for businesses in a competitive market. Transportation management ensures that companies meet customer expectations for timely and accurate deliveries. In industries where speed is a differentiator, like e-commerce, efficient transportation provides a competitive edge. Meeting customer delivery expectations can also drive brand loyalty and encourage repeat business.

1.3 Key Objectives of Transportation Management

The main objectives of transportation management are to enhance efficiency, manage costs, and ensure customer satisfaction. Each objective plays a vital role in the success of the overall transportation process.

1.3.1 Efficiency

Efficiency in transportation management involves optimizing resources and processes to achieve the highest possible output with the lowest input. Companies focus on consolidating shipments, planning optimal routes, and minimizing handling times. Transportation management systems (TMS) help organizations analyze and identify the most efficient transportation routes, carriers, and schedules to improve the speed and reliability of deliveries.

1.3.2 Cost Management

Cost management is a critical objective, as transportation can account for a substantial portion of supply chain expenses. Efficient transportation management seeks to reduce costs through strategic planning and execution. This might involve negotiating with carriers for favorable rates, selecting cost-effective modes of transport, consolidating loads, or employing technology to track fuel consumption. Effective cost management in transportation ultimately reduces overall supply chain costs, increasing profitability.

1.3.3 Customer Satisfaction

Meeting customer expectations is central to transportation management. Customers value timely deliveries, visibility into the status of their shipments, and the reliability of products arriving in good condition. In transportation management, achieving high levels of customer satisfaction entails efficient, transparent, and responsive service. Companies employ real-time tracking and proactive communication to keep customers informed and manage expectations.

1.4 Types of Transportation Modes

Transportation can occur through several modes, each with distinct advantages and disadvantages. The choice of mode often depends on factors like product type, distance, cost, and required delivery speed.

1.4.1 Road Transportation

Road transportation, or trucking, is the most widely used mode for transporting goods, particularly in domestic markets. It is flexible, enabling point-to-point movement of goods. Trucks can carry a variety of cargo types, from small parcels to large freight, and can easily accommodate adjustments in routes and schedules. However, road transportation is limited by fuel costs, traffic conditions, and environmental regulations.

Advantages of Road Transportation

Flexibility and accessibility: Trucks can reach areas that other modes cannot.

Suitable for short- to medium-distance shipments.

Easily adaptable to changes in demand or routing.

Disadvantages of Road Transportation

Vulnerability to traffic congestion and weather conditions.

Higher costs for long-distance or heavy cargo.

Limited load capacity compared to other modes like rail or sea.

1.4.2 Rail Transportation

Rail transportation is ideal for heavy, bulky, or high-volume shipments over long distances, particularly in regions with established rail networks. It is cost-effective and has a lower environmental impact than road or air transportation. However, rail networks are fixed, making it less flexible for door-to-door delivery, which often requires supplementary road transport.

Advantages of Rail Transportation

Cost-efficient for large shipments over long distances.

Lower fuel consumption and carbon emissions.

Reliable schedules not affected by road traffic.

Disadvantages of Rail Transportation

Limited flexibility, requiring additional handling and transfers.

Slower than air transportation for long distances.

Dependent on the availability of rail infrastructure.

1.4.3 Air Transportation

Air transportation is the fastest mode and is typically used for high-value, time-sensitive, or perishable goods. It supports rapid movement over long distances, connecting suppliers and customers globally. However, air transport is expensive and has a significant carbon footprint, which may not align with some companies' sustainability goals.

Advantages of Air Transportation

Speed: Ideal for time-sensitive shipments.

Extensive global reach, connecting distant markets.

Secure, with low risk of cargo damage.

Disadvantages of Air Transportation

High costs, making it suitable mainly for high-value or urgent goods.

Restricted by airport locations and flight schedules.

Environmental impact due to high fuel consumption.

1.4.4 Sea Transportation

Sea transportation is the primary mode for global trade, capable of handling large quantities of goods at lower costs. Ocean freight is cost-effective and suited for non-perishable, bulk, or heavy cargo like raw materials. However, it is the slowest mode, and delays at ports or weather issues can affect reliability.

Advantages of Sea Transportation

Cost-efficient for international shipments, particularly for bulk goods.

High capacity, handling large and heavy items.

More environmentally friendly per ton-mile compared to air.

Disadvantages of Sea Transportation

Long transit times, unsuitable for time-sensitive shipments.

Susceptible to weather disruptions and port congestion.

Additional costs for loading, unloading, and customs clearance.

1.4.5 Pipeline Transportation

Pipeline transportation is a specialized mode used primarily for liquid or gas commodities, such as oil, natural gas, and water. It is cost-effective for continuous, high-volume transportation over fixed routes. Once pipelines are established, they offer a reliable and environmentally friendly mode of transportation. However, pipelines have limited flexibility and high initial setup costs.

Advantages of Pipeline Transportation

Low operational costs and environmental impact.

Reliable, with continuous flow once established.

Reduces road congestion by handling large volumes.

Disadvantages of Pipeline Transportation

Limited to specific commodities like oil or gas.

High initial investment and restricted route flexibility.

Vulnerable to environmental concerns and regulatory restrictions.

Transportation management is a vital component of the supply chain, connecting the stages from raw materials to finished products. By understanding the various transportation modes and focusing on key objectives like efficiency, cost management, and customer satisfaction, companies can create effective transportation strategies that support their overall goals. As transportation continues to evolve with technological advancements, sustainability initiatives, and new market demands, mastering transportation management will remain essential for building resilient, efficient, and customer-centric supply chains.

Chapter 2: The Role of Transportation in Supply Chain Management

- **Transportation's Place in the Supply Chain**

- **Transportation's Impact on Cost and Lead Time**

- **Aligning Transportation with Business Strategy**

Transportation plays a crucial role in supply chain management, acting as the bridge between suppliers, manufacturers, distributors, and customers. It ensures the continuous movement of goods and helps companies meet demand in a timely and efficient manner. This chapter explores transportation's place in the supply chain, its impact on cost and lead time, and the importance of aligning transportation with broader business strategies to maximize effectiveness and support organizational goals.

2.1 Transportation's Place in the Supply Chain

Transportation is a critical element of logistics that connects each component of the supply chain. From sourcing raw materials to delivering finished goods to customers, transportation enables the flow of products across various stages, ensuring that supply meets demand. In modern supply chains, the transportation function plays multiple roles, including:

2.1.1 Facilitating the Flow of Goods

In supply chains, transportation links each stage, allowing goods to move smoothly from suppliers to manufacturers, from manufacturers to distribution centers, and from distribution centers to retailers or customers. Without efficient transportation, the supply chain would face disruptions, leading to stockouts, backorders, or delays. A robust transportation network supports a streamlined flow of goods, helping companies respond quickly to market demands.

2.1.2 Bridging Geographical Distances

Global supply chains rely on transportation to bridge vast geographical distances. Companies today source raw materials from different countries, manufacture in diverse locations, and sell products worldwide. Transportation makes it possible to manage these complex supply chains and connect suppliers, manufacturers, and customers across regions and borders. This allows businesses to operate in a global marketplace and reach new markets efficiently.

2.1.3 Enabling Inventory Management

Effective transportation management directly impacts inventory levels and turnover rates. When transportation is reliable and predictable, companies can operate with leaner inventories, reducing holding costs. On the other hand, if transportation is inconsistent or delayed, companies may need to maintain higher safety stocks to mitigate the risk of stockouts. Thus, transportation influences inventory decisions, helping companies balance supply with demand while minimizing excess stock.

2.1.4 Supporting Just-in-Time (JIT) Production

Many organizations rely on Just-in-Time (JIT) production, which minimizes inventory levels by timing deliveries precisely to match production schedules. Efficient transportation is vital for JIT, as any delay can disrupt the production line and increase costs. With reliable transportation, companies can reduce inventory waste, lower storage costs, and streamline manufacturing processes, making transportation management essential for JIT and lean manufacturing.

2.2 Transportation's Impact on Cost and Lead Time

Transportation significantly affects the cost structure and lead times within the supply chain. These two factors, in turn, influence customer satisfaction, competitiveness, and profitability.

2.2.1 Transportation Costs and Their Components

Transportation costs are a substantial part of overall supply chain expenses, often ranging from 5% to 15% of a company's revenue, depending on industry and location. Key components of transportation costs include:

Freight Costs: The cost charged by carriers for moving goods, typically calculated based on distance, weight, volume, and mode of transportation.

Fuel Costs: Fuel represents a variable cost in transportation, often subject to price fluctuations, which can impact profitability.

Labor Costs: Driver wages, handling charges, and other labor-related expenses contribute to transportation costs.

Handling and Loading: Expenses associated with loading and unloading cargo, particularly if specialized equipment is required.

Administrative and Compliance Costs: Paperwork, insurance, customs, and regulatory compliance add additional costs to transportation, especially for international shipments.

Managing these expenses requires strategic planning to optimize transportation modes, routes, and consolidation of shipments. Transportation costs directly affect product pricing, with inefficient or costly transportation potentially leading to higher prices for customers.

2.2.2 The Impact of Transportation on Lead Time

Lead time is the time taken from placing an order to its delivery, influenced by various factors, including transportation speed, distance, and mode selection. Reducing lead times is crucial in supply chains where customer expectations for fast, reliable delivery are high. Transportation management aims to minimize lead time without compromising cost or quality, thus enhancing customer satisfaction.

Order Processing Time: Delays in processing or preparing shipments can extend lead time.

Transit Time: The actual time taken by a mode of transport to move goods between locations.

Customs and Regulatory Delays: In international trade, customs checks, inspections, and documentation can lengthen lead times.

Handling and Transfer Times: Multiple handling points, such as transfers between modes, add time to the overall lead time.

By optimizing transportation, companies can reduce lead time, meeting customer expectations for quicker delivery. For instance, using air transport instead of sea freight shortens delivery time but increases costs, highlighting the trade-off between speed and cost in transportation decisions.

2.3 Aligning Transportation with Business Strategy

Aligning transportation with a company's business strategy ensures that logistical efforts support broader goals, such as cost leadership, differentiation, and customer satisfaction. Transportation decisions must align with the company's competitive positioning and core objectives to maximize the supply chain's effectiveness and responsiveness.

2.3.1 Transportation's Role in Cost Leadership

For companies competing on cost leadership, transportation management focuses on reducing expenses and optimizing efficiency. Cost-driven transportation strategies might include:

Mode Selection: Choosing the most economical mode, such as rail or sea, over more expensive options like air, when speed is not essential.

Route Optimization: Reducing distance and avoiding costly toll routes to minimize expenses.

Carrier Negotiation: Negotiating favorable rates and establishing long-term contracts with carriers.

Load Consolidation: Combining multiple shipments into a single load to reduce the cost per unit.

Cost-focused strategies benefit from a comprehensive analysis of transportation expenses and prioritizing long-term partnerships with cost-effective carriers, which also helps companies maintain competitive pricing for customers.

2.3.2 Transportation for Differentiation and Customer Satisfaction

In industries where differentiation and customer satisfaction are essential, companies use transportation to offer faster, more reliable, and more personalized services. These strategies might involve:

Expedited Shipping: Offering faster options like same-day or next-day delivery, especially for high-value or time-sensitive products.

Real-Time Tracking and Visibility: Providing customers with tracking capabilities to enhance transparency and build trust.

Flexible Delivery Options: Allowing customers to choose delivery windows or locations, which improves convenience and satisfaction.

By prioritizing customer-centric transportation strategies, companies can build brand loyalty and offer a superior customer experience, helping them stand out in a competitive market.

2.3.3 Sustainability as a Strategic Priority

With rising awareness of environmental issues, many companies are integrating sustainability into their transportation strategies. Sustainable transportation aims to reduce the environmental footprint through measures like:

Reducing Emissions: Using energy-efficient vehicles, investing in electric fleets, or choosing lower-emission modes like rail.

Optimizing Fuel Consumption: Route planning to minimize travel distances, reduce fuel use, and lower carbon emissions.

Consolidating Shipments: Reducing the number of trips by maximizing vehicle capacity, which decreases emissions per unit transported.

Aligning transportation with sustainability objectives not only supports corporate social responsibility but also meets the expectations of environmentally-conscious consumers, creating brand value.

In today's complex and dynamic supply chain landscape, transportation plays a pivotal role, impacting costs, lead times, and customer satisfaction. By understanding transportation's place in the supply chain, managing its impact on costs and lead time, and aligning it with business strategy, companies can achieve a balanced, efficient, and responsive supply chain.

Chapter 3: Transportation Modes and Modal Selection

Characteristics of Different Transportation Modes

Advantages and Disadvantages of Each Mode

Factors Influencing Mode Selection (Cost, Speed, Distance, Cargo Type)

Effective transportation management relies on choosing the right mode of transportation to ensure goods move swiftly, safely, and economically from origin to destination. With diverse options like road, rail, air, sea, and pipeline, each mode offers unique characteristics, benefits, and challenges. This chapter provides an overview of these modes, explores the advantages and disadvantages of each, and outlines key factors influencing mode selection, such as cost, speed, distance, and cargo type. We will also review case studies demonstrating how companies effectively select transportation modes based on their specific needs.

3.1 Characteristics of Different Transportation Modes

Transportation modes serve distinct roles within supply chains, each characterized by unique capabilities and limitations. Understanding these characteristics helps businesses select the mode that best meets their operational, budgetary, and customer requirements.

3.1.1 Road Transportation

Road transportation involves the use of trucks and other vehicles to transport goods via highways and local roads. It is the most flexible mode, allowing for door-to-door delivery and easy access to various regions, especially within national borders.

Typical Speed: Moderate

Flexibility: High, with door-to-door service capability

Suitable Cargo Types: Diverse, from consumer goods to perishables

Limitations: Limited load capacity, susceptible to traffic congestion, weather disruptions

3.1.2 Rail Transportation

Rail transport is a suitable option for moving large volumes of heavy or bulky goods over land, especially over long distances. Railways are energy-efficient and offer considerable cost advantages, especially for domestic freight.

Typical Speed: Moderate to high, depending on network efficiency

Flexibility: Limited to routes covered by railway lines

Suitable Cargo Types: Bulk goods, such as coal, minerals, and grain

Limitations: Limited geographic reach (requires access to rail infrastructure), slower delivery times compared to road for short distances

3.1.3 Air Transportation

Air transport is the fastest mode, ideal for time-sensitive and high-value cargo. However, it is also the most expensive, making it less suitable for bulky or low-cost goods.

Typical Speed: Very high

Flexibility: Limited to airports and requires secondary transport to complete last-mile delivery

Suitable Cargo Types: High-value, perishable, and time-sensitive goods (e.g., electronics, pharmaceuticals)

Limitations: High costs, limited cargo space, and environmental concerns due to high emissions

3.1.4 Sea Transportation

Sea transport, involving the use of ships, is essential for international trade and is the most cost-effective option for long-distance transport of large volumes of goods. It is particularly suitable for bulk and heavy items.

Typical Speed: Slow

Flexibility: Limited to ports and requires land transport to complete the delivery

Suitable Cargo Types: Bulk goods, machinery, automobiles, and other heavy or non-perishable items

Limitations: Long transit times, dependency on port infrastructure, and susceptibility to weather conditions

3.1.5 Pipeline Transportation

Pipelines are primarily used for transporting liquids and gases over long distances. Pipelines provide consistent, reliable transport with low operational costs after the initial setup but lack flexibility in terms of the type of cargo.

Typical Speed: Constant, depending on pipeline pressure and flow

Flexibility: Minimal, with a fixed infrastructure and limited to specific goods (e.g., oil, gas, chemicals)

Suitable Cargo Types: Liquids, gases, and certain chemicals

Limitations: High installation costs, limited to specific industries, and environmental concerns in case of leaks

3.2 Advantages and Disadvantages of Each Mode

Each transportation mode has unique advantages and disadvantages, which can significantly affect operational performance, costs, and customer satisfaction.

Mode	Advantages	Disadvantages
Road	Flexibility, door-to-door service, wide accessibility	Vulnerable to traffic delays, limited capacity
Rail	Cost-effective for bulk goods, energy-efficient	Limited reach, requires infrastructure
Air	Fastest mode, suitable for high-value/time-sensitive cargo	High cost, limited space, environmental impact
Sea	Cost-effective for large volumes, ideal for international trade	Long transit time, port dependency, environmental concerns
Pipeline	Low operational cost, consistent transport for liquids/gases	High initial cost, limited to specific industries, inflexible

3.3 Factors Influencing Mode Selection

Selecting an appropriate transportation mode involves evaluating various factors based on organizational priorities, budget, and product requirements. Key factors influencing mode selection include cost, speed, distance, and cargo type.

3.3.1 Cost

Cost is often the primary factor in mode selection, with companies aiming to minimize transportation expenses without compromising quality or reliability. Each mode varies significantly in cost: air transport is the most expensive, while sea, rail, and pipelines offer cost advantages for bulk transport. A comprehensive cost analysis helps companies choose the most economically viable option, particularly for routine or large-volume shipments.

3.3.2 Speed

Speed is crucial for time-sensitive goods, perishable items, and products with short lead times. Air transport offers the fastest option, making it ideal for expedited shipping and urgent orders. On the other hand, rail and sea transport, while slower, can be optimized for non-urgent shipments, particularly when planning for steady demand.

3.3.3 Distance

Distance influences mode choice, as certain modes are more effective for particular distances. For example, road transport is optimal for short to medium distances, while rail is preferable for longer domestic routes. Air and sea transport are essential for international shipments, with sea favored for transcontinental shipments due to cost-efficiency.

3.3.4 Cargo Type and Value

The nature of the cargo is a crucial consideration. Perishable goods, fragile items, and high-value goods typically require faster and more controlled transportation modes, such as air. Meanwhile, bulk commodities, low-cost goods, or products with extended shelf lives are more suited to slower modes like sea or rail. Pipelines are reserved for liquids, gases, and chemicals, making them suitable only for industries handling these materials.

3.3.5 Environmental Impact

Sustainability is increasingly influencing transportation decisions as companies aim to reduce carbon footprints. Environmentally conscious companies may favor rail over road transport for domestic shipments or sea over air for international trade, as these modes are more energy-efficient and emit less carbon.

3.4 Case Studies on Effective Mode Selection

Examining real-world cases of effective mode selection offers insight into how organizations balance cost, speed, and other factors to meet supply chain goals.

Case Study 1: Fast Fashion Industry and Air Transport

The fast fashion industry relies on short lead times to bring the latest trends to market quickly. To achieve this, companies often use air transport to move high-demand, low-weight items from overseas manufacturers to distribution centers and stores. Despite the high cost, air freight enables fast fashion companies to keep up with trends, reduce inventory holding costs, and maximize profitability.

Case Study 2: Bulk Commodities and Rail Transport in North America

In North America, rail is frequently chosen for transporting bulk commodities like coal, grain, and chemicals. Rail's cost-effectiveness, combined with the continent's extensive rail network, makes it ideal for these heavy, non-perishable products. One notable example is the agricultural sector, where crops are moved via rail from farming regions to processing centers and export ports, reducing reliance on road transport and achieving economies of scale.

Case Study 3: E-commerce and Multi-Modal Transport

E-commerce giants often employ a multi-modal transportation strategy to optimize speed and cost. An example is Amazon, which uses air for expedited deliveries, rail for cross-country transport of inventory, and road for last-mile delivery. By strategically choosing modes based on factors like location, cost, and customer delivery expectations, Amazon has established a highly efficient, responsive supply chain that enhances customer satisfaction.

Case Study 4: Oil and Gas Industry and Pipeline Transport

The oil and gas industry heavily relies on pipelines to transport crude oil, natural gas, and refined products across vast distances. Pipelines are the most efficient mode for these commodities, providing continuous, low-cost transport and reducing the need for alternative modes that could be more environmentally disruptive. Pipeline infrastructure is particularly valuable for high-volume, repetitive shipments, as it ensures consistent flow without the need for frequent handling.

Understanding the characteristics, advantages, and disadvantages of each transportation mode is essential for making informed decisions in supply chain management. Factors like cost, speed, cargo type, and environmental impact play critical roles in mode selection, as companies strive to balance operational efficiency with customer satisfaction. By strategically aligning mode choices with organizational priorities, businesses can enhance their supply chain's performance and resilience, positioning themselves competitively in the marketplace. The case studies presented demonstrate how companies across different industries effectively utilize transportation modes to achieve specific goals, from cost reduction to rapid delivery, underscoring the importance of thoughtful mode selection in modern supply chain management.

Chapter 4: Route Planning and Optimization

Principles of Route Planning

Tools and Techniques for Optimization

Minimizing Costs and Lead Times

Case Studies on Successful Route Optimization

Efficient route planning and optimization are essential components of transportation management, impacting costs, lead times, and customer satisfaction. By strategically planning transportation routes, businesses can streamline delivery schedules, reduce fuel consumption, and enhance overall efficiency. This chapter delves into the principles of route planning, examines tools and techniques for optimization, explores methods for minimizing costs and lead times, and includes case studies that illustrate successful route optimization strategies.

4.1 Principles of Route Planning

Route planning is the process of determining the most efficient paths for transporting goods from one point to another. Effective route planning considers factors such as distance, traffic conditions, fuel costs, delivery windows, and vehicle capacity. Below are the primary principles that guide route planning:

Efficiency: The goal is to select routes that minimize travel time and costs, ideally reducing the overall distance and fuel consumption.

Reliability: Consistent and dependable delivery times are crucial for meeting customer expectations and maintaining supply chain fluidity.

Flexibility: Good route planning must adapt to changing conditions, such as weather disruptions, traffic delays, or vehicle breakdowns.

Compliance: Routes should comply with regulations like road weight limits, hours-of-service laws, and environmental regulations to avoid penalties and legal issues.

Sustainability: Increasingly, companies aim to incorporate eco-friendly practices into route planning, selecting paths that reduce fuel consumption and carbon emissions.

Key Factors in Route Planning:

Distance and Geography: The shortest path is not always the most efficient, particularly in urban areas where traffic and road conditions play significant roles.

Delivery Windows: Many clients specify time windows for deliveries, adding constraints to route planning that require precise timing and sequencing.

Capacity and Load: Route planning must account for vehicle capacity to avoid overloading or underutilization, both of which affect operational costs.

Driver Availability: Driver scheduling, including mandatory rest periods, influences route planning. Efficient scheduling ensures that drivers are neither overworked nor underutilized.

4.2 Tools and Techniques for Optimization

Optimizing transportation routes goes beyond simply choosing the shortest path. It involves sophisticated algorithms and technologies to balance cost, time, and other constraints. Today, many businesses use advanced software and techniques to enhance route planning and achieve operational efficiencies.

4.2.1 Geographic Information Systems (GIS)

GIS technology enables route planners to visualize geographic data and make more informed decisions about route selection. By mapping out infrastructure, traffic patterns, and environmental factors, GIS tools offer insights into potential obstacles and help create optimized paths.

4.2.2 Routing and Scheduling Software

Specialized software, such as TMS (Transportation Management Systems), integrates routing, scheduling, and dispatching functions. These tools consider variables like delivery time windows, driver availability, vehicle capacity, and customer requirements to provide optimized route plans. Examples of popular route optimization software include Descartes, Route4Me, and Verizon Connect.

4.2.3 Artificial Intelligence and Machine Learning

AI and machine learning can improve route planning by analyzing historical data to predict future patterns. Machine learning algorithms learn from past traffic data, delays, and driver performance to continuously refine and improve route recommendations, even adapting to real-time conditions.

4.2.4 Real-Time GPS Tracking

Real-time GPS tracking is essential for dynamic routing, allowing companies to adjust routes based on live traffic, weather conditions, and unexpected disruptions. For instance, if a road closure or traffic congestion occurs, GPS tracking enables real-time rerouting to avoid delays and maintain delivery schedules.

4.2.5 Optimization Algorithms

Common algorithms used in route optimization include:

The Traveling Salesman Problem (TSP): This algorithm calculates the shortest possible route that visits each location once and returns to the origin point.

Vehicle Routing Problem (VRP): VRP extends TSP by including multiple vehicles with various capacities and constraints, helping planners determine the optimal assignment of routes to each vehicle.

Genetic Algorithms: Inspired by natural selection, these algorithms test various route combinations, "evolving" the best route over multiple iterations.

Heuristic Methods: These techniques provide quick solutions for complex routing problems by offering approximate answers instead of exact solutions, which can be useful for large fleets or complex delivery requirements.

4.3 Minimizing Costs and Lead Times

Cost and time are two of the most critical factors in transportation management. Effective route optimization can reduce operational expenses while maintaining or even shortening delivery lead times. Below are strategies for minimizing both costs and lead times through optimized route planning:

4.3.1 Reducing Fuel Costs

Fuel expenses account for a significant portion of transportation costs. By choosing efficient routes that minimize distance and avoid congested areas, companies can reduce fuel consumption. Techniques such as limiting idling times, reducing unnecessary detours, and maintaining optimal speeds further contribute to fuel efficiency.

4.3.2 Minimizing Empty Miles

Empty miles, or non-revenue-generating trips, increase operational costs without providing value. Effective route planning maximizes vehicle capacity and minimizes empty return trips, often by scheduling pickups along return routes or using backhaul strategies to fill vehicles on the way back.

4.3.3 Enhancing Delivery Speed and Consistency

Consistent delivery times are essential for customer satisfaction. By using real-time data and predictive algorithms, companies can preemptively identify delays and adjust routes. Advanced routing solutions also factor in delivery windows, so drivers adhere to specific time frames, increasing delivery reliability.

4.3.4 Implementing Multi-Stop Routes

For companies with multiple deliveries in close geographic proximity, multi-stop routing can drastically reduce travel time and costs. Software-based multi-stop route planning sequences deliveries in the most logical order, reducing the overall distance and minimizing fuel usage.

4.3.5 Leveraging Data for Continuous Improvement

Data analytics play an essential role in identifying inefficiencies and areas for improvement in route planning. By examining data on past deliveries, companies can identify frequent bottlenecks, peak traffic times, and high-cost routes, adjusting their planning accordingly.

4.4 Case Studies on Successful Route Optimization

The following case studies highlight companies that successfully optimized their transportation routes, demonstrating tangible benefits such as reduced costs, shorter lead times, and enhanced customer satisfaction.

Case Study 1: UPS and Advanced Routing Algorithms

UPS is renowned for its commitment to route optimization, primarily through the use of its proprietary routing software, ORION (On-Road Integrated Optimization and Navigation). ORION optimizes delivery routes based on factors like traffic patterns, customer delivery windows, and vehicle capacity. Notably, UPS drivers are instructed to avoid left turns, which reduces idling time and fuel consumption by minimizing time spent waiting to cross traffic. By implementing ORION, UPS saves millions of gallons of fuel annually, reduces emissions, and enhances delivery speed, setting a benchmark in transportation efficiency.

Case Study 2: Coca-Cola's Multi-Stop Delivery Optimization

Coca-Cola optimized its delivery routes using route planning software that enabled multi-stop scheduling. The software sequenced deliveries to reduce the distance traveled between customer locations, maximizing each vehicle's capacity. As a result, Coca-Cola was able to minimize operational costs, reduce delivery lead times, and decrease its carbon footprint by limiting unnecessary mileage. This strategic approach helped Coca-Cola enhance its delivery efficiency, especially in urban areas where multiple clients are located close to one another.

Case Study 3: Amazon's Dynamic Routing with Real-Time Data

Amazon utilizes a dynamic routing system that leverages real-time data from GPS and traffic sensors to constantly adjust routes for its delivery drivers. By monitoring live traffic conditions, Amazon's routing software adapts to changing conditions, such as road closures or peak traffic periods, ensuring that drivers take the most efficient path possible. This system is particularly effective in urban areas, where traffic congestion can significantly impact delivery schedules. The dynamic routing solution enables Amazon to meet its ambitious same-day and next-day delivery promises, enhancing customer satisfaction.

Case Study 4: Walmart's Last-Mile Delivery Optimization

Walmart adopted a technology-driven approach to optimize its last-mile delivery routes, using advanced routing algorithms and real-time tracking. Walmart's system integrates data on traffic, delivery windows, and customer locations, allowing for route adjustments on the fly. The last-mile optimization strategy reduces delivery costs, speeds up deliveries, and minimizes fuel consumption, making it easier for Walmart to maintain competitive pricing and service levels in the growing online retail market.

Route planning and optimization are fundamental for efficient and cost-effective transportation management. By employing a combination of advanced tools and techniques, businesses can significantly reduce travel time, lower operational costs, and enhance service reliability. From geographic information systems to real-time GPS tracking and sophisticated algorithms, the tools available for route optimization empower companies to achieve their strategic transportation goals. The case studies of UPS, Coca-Cola, Amazon, and Walmart demonstrate how different organizations across industries have successfully leveraged route optimization to improve efficiency and meet customer demands.

Through strategic route planning, businesses not only enhance their supply chain performance but also contribute to sustainable practices by reducing emissions and fuel consumption. Ultimately, effective route optimization is a critical asset for companies striving to remain competitive in an increasingly complex and fast-paced market.

Chapter 5: Fleet Management and Maintenance

Types of Fleets and Fleet Composition

Fleet Maintenance Best Practices

Fuel Efficiency and Environmental Impact

Innovations in Fleet Management (Electric and Autonomous Vehicles)

Fleet management is a cornerstone of transportation management, ensuring that a company's vehicles are effectively utilized, well-maintained, and environmentally efficient. In today's rapidly evolving transportation landscape, advancements in fleet technology and a growing emphasis on sustainability have reshaped how businesses approach fleet management. This chapter discusses the types of fleets and their composition, best practices in fleet maintenance, strategies for improving fuel efficiency and minimizing environmental impact, and emerging innovations like electric and autonomous vehicles.

5.1 Types of Fleets and Fleet Composition

Fleet composition refers to the selection and combination of different types of vehicles within a company's fleet, tailored to meet specific operational needs. Fleet managers must carefully consider vehicle types, sizes, and capabilities to optimize performance and control costs.

5.1.1 Types of Fleets

There are several types of fleets, each serving distinct purposes within supply chain operations. Key fleet types include:

Freight Fleets: Primarily composed of trucks, trailers, and other large vehicles designed for transporting goods over long distances. These fleets may include specialized vehicles like flatbeds, refrigerated trucks, and tankers, depending on the type of cargo.

Service Fleets: Used by companies that provide on-site services such as utility companies, repair services, or healthcare providers. These fleets typically include vans, utility trucks, or specialized vehicles equipped with tools and equipment.

Delivery Fleets: Focused on last-mile logistics, these fleets deliver products directly to customers, often in urban areas. Delivery fleets generally include smaller vehicles such as vans and box trucks.

Leased and Rental Fleets: Many companies choose to lease or rent their fleets to reduce the cost and responsibility of ownership. Leased and rental fleets can include various vehicle types, often offering flexibility for seasonal or project-based operations.

5.1.2 Fleet Composition Considerations

When building a fleet, companies need to evaluate the specific needs of their operations, including cargo type, delivery frequency, distance, and fuel efficiency. Fleet composition should be flexible enough to adapt to fluctuations in demand while minimizing costs. Factors to consider when assembling a fleet include:

Vehicle Size and Capacity: Selecting vehicles with appropriate capacity reduces trips, fuel usage, and wear on equipment. Overloading or underutilizing vehicles can drive up costs.

Vehicle Type: Specialized vehicles (e.g., refrigerated trucks for perishable goods) ensure cargo arrives in optimal condition, while general-purpose vehicles provide flexibility across various goods.

Operational Range: Long-haul transportation may require larger trucks, while urban delivery is better suited to smaller, more maneuverable vehicles.

5.2 Fleet Maintenance Best Practices

Regular fleet maintenance is crucial to ensure vehicle safety, extend service life, and minimize downtime. Preventative maintenance, in particular, allows companies to avoid unexpected breakdowns, reduce repair costs, and keep vehicles operating at peak efficiency.

5.2.1 Preventive Maintenance Programs

Preventive maintenance (PM) involves routine inspections and servicing at scheduled intervals to prevent mechanical failures. A well-structured PM program typically includes oil changes, tire inspections, brake checks, and engine diagnostics.

Scheduled Inspections: Routine inspections allow fleet managers to identify and address wear-and-tear issues before they escalate into costly repairs.

Predictive Maintenance: Using data analytics and sensor technology, predictive maintenance monitors vehicle performance and anticipates potential issues based on usage patterns and real-time data, reducing downtime and improving reliability.

Maintenance Documentation: Keeping accurate maintenance records provides insights into vehicle performance, repair history, and helps identify recurring issues. Documentation also ensures compliance with safety regulations.

5.2.2 Maintenance Best Practices

Effective fleet maintenance involves more than just following a checklist. Best practices include:

Prioritizing Safety: Regular checks of critical systems such as brakes, tires, and lights are essential for maintaining safety standards.

Optimizing Repair Schedules: Fleet managers should coordinate repair schedules to minimize disruption. For instance, maintenance can be done during off-peak hours to keep vehicles available during busy times.

Training Drivers: Educating drivers on vehicle operation, basic maintenance, and reporting issues early can prevent minor issues from becoming major problems.

Leveraging Maintenance Software: Many fleet management systems now include maintenance tracking capabilities, making it easier for managers to schedule and monitor maintenance activities, track costs, and anticipate repair needs.

5.3 Fuel Efficiency and Environmental Impact

Fuel consumption is one of the highest operating costs in transportation, and reducing it not only saves money but also benefits the environment by reducing greenhouse gas emissions. Fleet managers are increasingly focused on fuel-efficient practices and alternative fuels to mitigate environmental impact.

5.3.1 Strategies for Fuel Efficiency

Improving fuel efficiency can be achieved through various approaches, such as:

Route Optimization: Planning efficient routes minimizes unnecessary mileage and fuel use. As discussed in Chapter 4, tools like GPS tracking and AI-based routing help reduce idle time and avoid congested routes.

Speed Control: Driving at optimal speeds reduces fuel consumption. Speed governors can be installed to prevent drivers from exceeding fuel-efficient speed ranges.

Idle Reduction: Idling wastes fuel and increases emissions. Anti-idling policies, along with automatic engine shut-off technology, prevent vehicles from idling unnecessarily.

Load Optimization: Ensuring vehicles are loaded to their optimal weight capacity reduces the number of trips required, saving fuel and reducing emissions.

5.3.2 Reducing Environmental Impact

Sustainability is becoming a priority for businesses, leading to initiatives aimed at reducing fleet emissions. Options include:

Low-Emission and Alternative Fuel Vehicles: Many companies are adopting vehicles that use cleaner fuels, such as compressed natural gas (CNG), liquefied natural gas (LNG), or propane. Hybrid and fully electric vehicles are increasingly viable options as technology advances.

Carbon Offsetting: Companies can offset their emissions by investing in carbon reduction projects, such as reforestation or renewable energy.

Sustainability Metrics and Reporting: Tracking and reporting emissions provide insight into a fleet's environmental impact, helping companies set goals for emission reduction and measure progress.

5.4 Innovations in Fleet Management (Electric and Autonomous Vehicles)

Technological advancements in fleet management are revolutionizing the industry, with innovations like electric vehicles (EVs) and autonomous vehicles (AVs) promising to reshape transportation by enhancing efficiency, reducing environmental impact, and lowering operating costs.

5.4.1 Electric Vehicles (EVs)

Electric vehicles are gaining popularity due to their low operational costs and environmental benefits. While EVs have higher upfront costs, they offer long-term savings in fuel and maintenance. Key considerations for implementing EVs in fleets include:

Battery Range and Charging Infrastructure: EV range has improved significantly, making them suitable for urban delivery fleets and short-haul routes. However, the availability of charging stations and charging time constraints are important factors for fleet managers.

Cost Savings: EVs reduce fuel expenses and generally have lower maintenance costs due to fewer moving parts and lower wear and tear.

Sustainability Impact: EVs produce zero tailpipe emissions, helping companies meet sustainability goals and reduce their carbon footprint.

5.4.2 Autonomous Vehicles (AVs)

Autonomous or self-driving vehicles are still in the early stages of commercial adoption but have the potential to transform fleet management by increasing safety, efficiency, and operational flexibility.

Enhanced Safety: AVs can reduce accidents caused by driver error, thereby improving safety and reducing liability for companies.

Operational Efficiency: AVs could allow fleets to operate around the clock, as driver availability and rest periods become irrelevant. This can improve delivery times and decrease labor costs.

Challenges and Limitations: The adoption of AVs faces regulatory challenges, technological limitations, and public acceptance hurdles. Additionally, the initial investment for autonomous technology is high, which may limit accessibility for some companies.

5.4.3 Telematics and IoT in Fleet Management

Telematics systems use sensors and IoT technology to collect data on vehicle performance, location, and driver behavior. This data provides valuable insights that help improve fleet efficiency, safety, and maintenance planning.

Real-Time Tracking: Telematics enables real-time vehicle tracking, providing fleet managers with location data, route progress, and estimated delivery times.

Predictive Maintenance: Telematics data allows for predictive maintenance by alerting fleet managers to issues like declining engine performance or low tire pressure before they become serious problems.

Driver Behavior Monitoring: Telematics can track driver habits, such as speeding or harsh braking, allowing for targeted training to improve safety and fuel efficiency.

Conclusion

Fleet management and maintenance are critical components of transportation operations, requiring careful planning, adherence to best practices, and strategic adoption of new technologies. By optimizing fleet composition, implementing preventive maintenance programs, and focusing on fuel efficiency, companies can reduce operational costs and improve reliability.

Innovations in fleet management, including electric and autonomous vehicles, promise exciting opportunities for the future, enabling companies to further reduce their environmental impact and achieve greater efficiency. However, these technologies also come with challenges and considerations, from infrastructure needs to regulatory compliance. As fleet management continues to evolve, companies must stay informed about new developments and adapt their strategies to remain competitive and sustainable in an ever-changing market.

Chapter 6: Transportation Costs and Pricing Strategies

Cost Components in Transportation

Calculating Transportation Costs

Pricing Models (Freight Rates, Surcharges)

Strategies for Cost Reduction

Efficient cost management is essential in transportation, as it directly affects an organization's profitability and competitiveness. Transportation costs include fuel, labor, maintenance, and other operational expenses, which add up quickly in logistics and supply chain management. In this chapter, we will examine the primary components of transportation costs, methods for calculating these expenses, commonly used pricing models, and strategies that organizations can adopt to control and reduce transportation costs effectively.

6.1 Cost Components in Transportation

Understanding the breakdown of transportation costs is the first step toward managing and optimizing them. Transportation costs are influenced by several variable and fixed components, which can vary by mode, route, and business model.

6.1.1 Fixed and Variable Costs

Fixed Costs: These are costs that do not change with the volume of goods transported. Examples include vehicle leasing or depreciation, facility costs for storage, and salaries for drivers and support staff. Fixed costs are typically easier to predict and budget for, making them stable expenses in transportation operations.

Variable Costs: Variable costs fluctuate based on the volume of goods, distance traveled, and other operational factors. Fuel, tolls, vehicle maintenance, and repair are examples of variable costs. These can vary widely depending on economic conditions (e.g., fuel prices) and external factors like traffic or weather.

6.1.2 Key Cost Drivers in Transportation

Several factors drive transportation costs, impacting both fixed and variable expenses:

Fuel Costs: Fuel is one of the most significant components of transportation costs. Changes in fuel prices, driven by market conditions or geopolitical events, can significantly impact total transportation expenses.

Labor Costs: Wages for drivers and logistics personnel contribute to transportation costs. For companies facing driver shortages, labor costs can escalate, as higher wages may be necessary to attract qualified drivers.

Maintenance and Repair: Vehicle maintenance and repairs are critical to ensure safe and reliable operations. Preventative maintenance can help control these costs, but unexpected repairs can lead to cost spikes.

Tolls and Taxes: Tolls, permits, and taxes associated with using certain highways, bridges, or tunnels can increase transportation expenses. In some regions, congestion charges or environmental fees may also apply.

Insurance: Fleet insurance is essential for risk management, especially in cases of accidents or cargo loss. Premiums may vary depending on the type of vehicles, routes, and risk profile.

6.1.3 Mode-Specific Cost Considerations

Different modes of transportation (road, rail, air, sea, and pipeline) each come with unique cost considerations:

Road Transportation: This mode incurs high fuel, labor, and maintenance costs but offers flexibility and convenience.

Rail Transportation: Generally more fuel-efficient for long-haul shipments, rail costs include railcar fees, maintenance of rail infrastructure, and switching fees at terminals.

Air Transportation: Airfreight is the most expensive mode due to high fuel costs and airport fees but is often chosen for high-value or time-sensitive goods.

Sea Transportation: Fuel costs, port fees, and cargo handling are the primary costs for maritime transport. Sea transport is cost-effective for bulk shipments but has a longer transit time.

Pipeline Transportation: Pipeline transport is cost-effective for liquids and gases over long distances but requires high initial investment and regular maintenance costs.

6.2 Calculating Transportation Costs

Accurate cost calculations are essential for managing budgets and identifying opportunities for cost reduction. Cost calculation methods vary based on the mode of transport, shipment details, and pricing structures.

6.2.1 Direct and Indirect Costs

Transportation costs are often divided into direct and indirect categories.

Direct Costs: These are directly related to each shipment, such as fuel expenses, labor for loading/unloading, and toll fees. Direct costs are easier to attribute to specific shipments.

Indirect Costs: These are shared across multiple shipments, including administrative expenses, facility upkeep, and fleet depreciation. Indirect costs require cost allocation methods to distribute expenses fairly among shipments.

6.2.2 Calculating Per-Mile or Per-Kilometer Costs

One of the most common methods for calculating transportation costs is on a per-mile or per-kilometer basis. This calculation provides insight into how much it costs to operate a vehicle for each mile or kilometer traveled. Factors influencing per-mile costs include fuel efficiency, driver wages, and vehicle depreciation.

6.2.3 Load Weight and Volume Calculations

When calculating transportation costs, load weight and volume play a significant role. Heavy or large-volume shipments may incur higher costs due to the impact on fuel consumption and the space they occupy.

6.3 Pricing Models in Transportation (Freight Rates, Surcharges)

Transportation companies use various pricing models to structure their rates, depending on factors such as distance, shipment weight, and market conditions. Understanding these pricing models can help businesses make informed decisions when selecting carriers.

6.3.1 Freight Rates

Freight rates represent the base cost of transporting goods and can vary widely by mode and distance. Common freight rate models include:

Flat Rate: This model charges a fixed price for transportation regardless of load weight or distance, typically used for short-haul deliveries or within specific regions.

Per Mile or Per Kilometer Rate: This rate model charges based on the distance traveled, common in long-haul trucking and rail transport. Rates may vary by weight and type of cargo.

Weight and Volume-Based Rate: Freight costs are calculated based on the shipment's weight or volume, particularly relevant for air and maritime transportation, where space is a premium.

6.3.2 Surcharges and Additional Fees

In addition to base freight rates, transportation providers may apply surcharges to cover fluctuating expenses or additional services.

Fuel Surcharge: Given the volatility of fuel prices, carriers often apply a fuel surcharge to protect against sudden price increases.

Peak Season Surcharge: During high-demand periods, such as holiday seasons, carriers may impose additional fees.

Handling and Accessorial Charges: Additional fees for services such as loading/unloading, waiting time, and access to restricted areas.

Environmental Surcharges: In some regions, carriers may apply green fees to offset emissions and promote sustainability efforts.

6.4 Strategies for Cost Reduction

Reducing transportation costs is a key objective in transportation management. By implementing strategic practices and leveraging technology, companies can lower expenses while maintaining service quality.

6.4.1 Route Optimization

One of the most effective strategies for cost reduction is route optimization, which minimizes mileage, fuel consumption, and time spent on the road. Route optimization software uses algorithms to calculate the most efficient routes, considering factors such as traffic patterns, delivery windows, and load constraints.

6.4.2 Consolidation and Load Optimization

Consolidating shipments and optimizing load capacity reduces the number of trips needed, which helps cut fuel and labor costs. This strategy is particularly effective for companies handling large volumes of goods with overlapping delivery destinations.

6.4.3 Collaboration and Shared Transportation

Collaboration with other companies to share transportation resources can lower costs. Shared transportation allows companies to consolidate shipments with partners, increasing load efficiency and reducing costs per shipment.

6.4.4 Fuel Management Programs

Fuel management programs focus on reducing fuel consumption through practices such as speed control, regular vehicle maintenance, and driver training. Monitoring fuel usage and setting reduction goals can help companies manage one of their largest variable costs.

6.4.5 Negotiating Carrier Contracts

Building strong relationships with carriers and negotiating favorable contracts can lead to cost savings. Companies can negotiate discounts based on shipment volume, delivery frequency, and seasonal adjustments. Additionally, long-term contracts can secure consistent pricing and protect against market fluctuations.

6.4.6 Technology and Automation

Technology plays a pivotal role in reducing transportation costs by streamlining processes and improving efficiency. Key technologies include:

Transportation Management Systems (TMS): TMS software assists in route planning, carrier selection, and load optimization, helping companies control costs more effectively.

Telematics and GPS Tracking: These tools provide real-time data on vehicle location, driver behavior, and fuel consumption, allowing for proactive cost management.

Automated Billing and Payment: Automation in billing and payment processes reduces administrative time and errors, ensuring cost accuracy and saving time.

6.4.7 Sustainable Practices for Cost Reduction

Sustainable practices can also contribute to long-term cost savings by reducing fuel consumption and environmental impact. Strategies include adopting energy-efficient vehicles, reducing idle time, and selecting carriers that use eco-friendly practices.

Transportation costs are a major part of supply chain expenses, and effective management of these costs is essential to maintaining profitability and competitiveness. By understanding the components that contribute to transportation costs, calculating costs accurately, and adopting strategic pricing and cost reduction methods, companies can manage transportation expenses more effectively.

From route optimization and fuel management to leveraging technology and sustainable practices, the strategies covered in this chapter provide actionable insights for reducing transportation costs while meeting business objectives. With a comprehensive approach to transportation cost management, companies can enhance their supply chain efficiency and drive sustainable growth in a competitive marketplace.

Chapter 7: Risk Management in Transportation

Types of Transportation Risks (Accidents, Delays, Theft, Weather)

Strategies for Risk Mitigation and Contingency Planning

Role of Insurance in Transportation

Case Studies on Managing Transportation Risks

Transportation plays a critical role in supply chain operations, but it is also inherently exposed to various risks that can disrupt the movement of goods. Effective risk management is essential for minimizing these disruptions and ensuring that goods are delivered safely, on time, and within budget. In this chapter, we will examine the types of transportation risks, explore strategies for mitigating these risks, discuss the role of insurance, and review case studies on managing transportation risks effectively.

7.1 Types of Transportation Risks

Transportation is vulnerable to several risk factors that can negatively impact supply chain operations. Understanding these risks is the first step in developing an effective risk management strategy.

7.1.1 Accidents

Accidents involving transportation vehicles (e.g., trucks, ships, trains) can lead to delays, cargo damage, and even loss of life. Road transportation, in particular, is prone to accidents due to traffic congestion, driver fatigue, and vehicle mechanical issues. Rail, air, and sea transport also face accident risks due to equipment failure, human error, and adverse weather conditions.

7.1.2 Delays

Delays are one of the most common and challenging risks in transportation. They can be caused by various factors, such as traffic congestion, port congestion, customs clearance issues, and strikes. Delays lead to increased costs, reduced customer satisfaction, and potential disruptions across the entire supply chain.

7.1.3 Theft and Security Breaches

Cargo theft and security breaches are major risks, especially for high-value goods. Theft can occur at various stages of transportation, such as at ports, in transit, or at distribution centers. Additionally, cyber threats targeting transportation management systems can lead to data breaches, shipment misrouting, and unauthorized access to cargo.

7.1.4 Weather-Related Risks

Adverse weather conditions, such as hurricanes, snowstorms, and heavy rainfall, can significantly impact transportation. For instance, severe weather can make roads impassable, delay flights, and disrupt port operations, leading to increased transit times and costs. Weather-related risks are particularly relevant for modes like sea and air transport, which are highly sensitive to environmental conditions.

7.1.5 Regulatory and Compliance Risks

Changes in regulations, such as new environmental standards, cargo handling requirements, or trade restrictions, can impact transportation costs and operations. Failure to comply with these regulations can result in fines, penalties, or even the suspension of transport activities.

7.2 Strategies for Risk Mitigation and Contingency Planning

Mitigating transportation risks requires a proactive approach, combining preventive measures, real-time monitoring, and contingency planning.

7.2.1 Preventive Measures

Preventive measures are essential to avoid risks and reduce their impact if they occur. Key preventive strategies include:

Driver Training and Safety Programs: Ensuring drivers are well-trained in safety protocols reduces accident risks. Regular training on safe driving, fatigue management, and defensive driving practices can help mitigate accident-related risks.

Vehicle Maintenance and Inspections: Regular maintenance of vehicles and equipment minimizes the chances of breakdowns and mechanical failures. Pre-trip inspections and preventive maintenance schedules help ensure that vehicles are in good working condition.

Cargo Security: To mitigate theft, companies can invest in cargo tracking devices, secure packaging, and high-security facilities. Using tamper-evident seals and minimizing stopovers also reduce the risk of theft during transit.

7.2.2 Real-Time Monitoring and Tracking

Implementing real-time monitoring and tracking systems allows companies to stay informed about the location and status of their shipments. GPS tracking, telematics, and

Internet of Things (IoT) devices provide valuable data on vehicle location, driver behavior, and environmental conditions. Real-time data helps logistics managers respond promptly to potential risks and take corrective actions.

7.2.3 Contingency Planning

Contingency planning is essential for preparing responses to unexpected disruptions. A comprehensive contingency plan includes:

Alternative Routes and Carriers: Identifying alternative transportation routes or backup carriers can reduce delays in case of disruptions. Route diversification ensures that companies have options if the primary route is affected by adverse conditions.

Emergency Communication Protocols: Establishing clear communication channels with drivers, logistics partners, and customers allows companies to relay updates promptly in the event of delays or incidents.

Inventory Buffering: Building buffer stocks or safety inventories near key distribution centers can mitigate the impact of transportation delays on customer service.

7.2.4 Insurance and Risk Transfer

Insurance plays a critical role in transferring financial risk associated with transportation incidents. Insurance coverage varies by mode, and policies can include cargo insurance, liability insurance, and business interruption insurance.

7.3 The Role of Insurance in Transportation

Insurance is a valuable tool for managing transportation risks, as it provides financial protection in case of accidents, theft, or other unexpected events. By transferring the risk to an insurance provider, companies can mitigate the financial impact of transportation-related incidents.

7.3.1 Types of Transportation Insurance

Cargo Insurance: Cargo insurance covers the value of goods during transit. This insurance can be all-risk, which covers a broad range of risks, or named-perils, which covers only specific risks listed in the policy.

Carrier Liability Insurance: This insurance covers the carrier's liability for damage or loss of cargo while in their custody. It does not cover all risks, so companies may need additional cargo insurance.

Vehicle and Driver Insurance: This type of insurance covers damage to the vehicle, driver injuries, and third-party liability in the case of an accident.

Business Interruption Insurance: For businesses heavily reliant on transportation, business interruption insurance provides coverage for income lost due to transportation disruptions.

7.3.2 Choosing the Right Insurance Policy

Choosing the right insurance policy requires understanding the specific risks associated with the goods, mode of transportation, and routes. Factors to consider include the cargo's value, susceptibility to theft or damage, and the likelihood of delays due to environmental or political factors. A comprehensive insurance policy should align with the company's overall risk management strategy.

7.4 Case Studies on Managing Transportation Risks

Examining real-world examples helps illustrate the practical application of risk management strategies in transportation.

Case Study 1: Managing Weather Risks in Maritime Transportation

A global electronics manufacturer faced frequent delays due to weather disruptions along key maritime routes. To address this, the company implemented an advanced weather monitoring system and established contingency plans with alternative ports. Additionally, it secured business interruption insurance to cover potential income losses due to delays. This approach allowed the company to reduce the impact of weather-related disruptions and meet customer expectations more consistently.

Case Study 2: Theft Prevention in Road Transportation

A high-end fashion retailer experienced multiple instances of cargo theft during road transportation. To mitigate this risk, the retailer implemented GPS tracking on its delivery trucks and adopted secure loading and unloading protocols. It also partnered with a logistics provider that specialized in high-security transportation services and required driver background checks. These steps reduced theft incidents, ensuring safer and more reliable delivery of goods.

Case Study 3: Addressing Regulatory Risks in Cross-Border Transportation

A food and beverage company frequently transported perishable goods across borders. Regulatory changes and customs delays posed significant risks. The company worked with a customs broker to ensure compliance with regulations and implemented a TMS (Transportation Management System) to monitor changes in customs requirements. As a result, it reduced the occurrence of customs delays and maintained the quality of its perishable products.

Case Study 4: Accident Risk Management in Trucking

A large retail chain suffered from high accident rates in its truck fleet, leading to delays and cargo damage. To address this issue, the company implemented a driver safety training program, equipped vehicles with telematics to monitor driver behavior, and incentivized safe driving practices. These changes resulted in a decrease in accidents, improved delivery times, and reduced insurance premiums.

Risk management in transportation is essential to maintain efficient, reliable, and cost-effective supply chain operations. By identifying the different types of transportation risks—such as accidents, delays, theft, weather, and regulatory challenges—companies can implement targeted strategies to mitigate these risks. Preventive measures, real-time monitoring, contingency planning, and insurance play vital roles in minimizing the impact of transportation disruptions.

As illustrated by the case studies, a proactive approach to risk management can reduce losses, improve customer satisfaction, and enhance operational resilience. By incorporating comprehensive risk management practices, companies can strengthen their transportation operations and ensure that their supply chains remain robust and adaptable in the face of uncertainty.

Chapter 8: Legal and Regulatory Considerations

Overview of Transportation Laws and Regulations

Compliance with National and International Laws

Customs, Tariffs, and Trade Regulations

Liability and Insurance Considerations

Effective transportation management goes beyond logistics and efficiency; it also requires a thorough understanding of the legal and regulatory landscape. Compliance with transportation laws and regulations is essential to protect companies from legal risks and financial penalties while ensuring smooth, uninterrupted operations. In this chapter, we'll discuss the foundational laws and regulations governing transportation, examine the importance of compliance, review key considerations surrounding customs and tariffs, and explore liability and insurance considerations for transportation managers.

8.1 Overview of Transportation Laws and Regulations

Transportation laws vary widely across countries, modes of transport, and specific types of cargo. These laws establish standards for safety, security, environmental protection, and fair business practices. Compliance is necessary not only to avoid legal repercussions but also to maintain a company's reputation, ensure customer satisfaction, and reduce operational risks.

8.1.1 Key Areas of Regulation in Transportation

Transportation regulations typically focus on several key areas:

Safety Standards: Governments regulate vehicle standards, driver qualifications, and maintenance requirements to promote safety and prevent accidents. For example, road transportation regulations often specify maximum driving hours and required rest periods to prevent fatigue-related accidents.

Environmental Regulations: Many countries have established laws to limit the environmental impact of transportation. These can include emissions standards, restrictions on fuel types, and waste disposal regulations for vehicles. Compliance with environmental laws is critical to support sustainability goals and avoid fines.

Security Regulations: For freight transportation, security measures aim to prevent theft, unauthorized access, and terrorism risks. For instance, the U.S. Customs and Border Protection (CBP) mandates advanced security protocols for international shipments.

Economic and Competitive Standards: Laws also govern fair pricing, competition, and market entry. In the European Union, for example, strict antitrust regulations prevent anti-competitive behavior, ensuring a level playing field in transportation services.

8.1.2 Major Regulatory Bodies

The agencies overseeing transportation vary by country and mode:

Federal Motor Carrier Safety Administration (FMCSA): In the U.S., the FMCSA oversees road transport, including trucking safety and compliance with operational standards.

International Maritime Organization (IMO): For maritime shipping, the IMO establishes global safety and environmental standards. The SOLAS (Safety of Life at Sea) Convention, for instance, requires containerized cargo to be accurately weighed and labeled.

International Civil Aviation Organization (ICAO): The ICAO establishes global aviation standards, including regulations for cargo safety and security on aircraft.

Customs and Border Agencies: Agencies like the CBP in the U.S., the General Administration of Customs in China, and the EU's customs departments regulate trade and enforce import/export rules.

8.2 Compliance with National and International Laws

Ensuring compliance with transportation regulations is a complex process, especially for businesses operating across multiple regions and using diverse transportation modes.

8.2.1 National vs. International Compliance

For domestic shipments, businesses must comply with national laws, such as vehicle safety standards, labor regulations, and insurance requirements. For international shipments, compliance is more complex due to varying international regulations, including trade restrictions, environmental standards, and import/export requirements.

8.2.2 Key Areas of Compliance in Transportation

Documentation and Labeling: All shipments must be accompanied by proper documentation, including bills of lading, packing lists, and certificates of origin. Accurate labeling is critical for compliance, particularly for hazardous materials.

Permits and Certifications: Some types of cargo, such as perishable goods or hazardous materials, require special permits and certifications. Businesses must ensure that all necessary permits are in place to avoid delays or legal issues.

Export Control and Trade Sanctions: Businesses shipping internationally must be aware of trade sanctions and export control regulations. Violating sanctions, such as those imposed by the U.S. Office of Foreign Assets Control (OFAC), can lead to severe penalties.

8.2.3 Challenges of Compliance

Managing compliance in transportation can be challenging due to the complex and often changing nature of laws. Technology can assist in tracking regulatory changes, automating documentation, and ensuring that all requirements are met. Additionally, many companies rely on customs brokers or third-party logistics (3PL) providers to handle compliance-related processes, especially in international logistics.

8.3 Customs, Tariffs, and Trade Regulations

Customs regulations and tariffs play a significant role in international transportation, affecting the cost and speed of shipments. Understanding these elements is essential for effective management of cross-border transportation.

8.3.1 Customs Clearance Process

Customs clearance is a crucial step in cross-border shipments, ensuring that goods comply with the laws of the importing country. During customs clearance, goods are examined to verify documentation, calculate applicable duties and taxes, and assess compliance with import regulations.

Documentation Required: Common documents include the commercial invoice, packing list, bill of lading, and certificate of origin. Missing or inaccurate documentation can lead to delays, fines, or shipment rejection.

Customs Duties and Taxes: Import duties and taxes are imposed on goods entering a country, often based on the value of the shipment, type of goods, and country of origin. Customs duties can vary widely and impact the overall cost of transportation.

8.3.2 Understanding Tariffs and Trade Agreements

Tariffs and trade agreements significantly impact transportation costs:

Tariffs: Tariffs are taxes imposed on imported goods, often calculated as a percentage of the goods' value. High tariffs can make imported goods more expensive and affect demand. Tariffs can also influence the choice of transportation routes to minimize duties.

Trade Agreements: Trade agreements, such as the United States-Mexico-Canada Agreement (USMCA) and the European Union's trade agreements, often reduce or eliminate tariffs, making cross-border transportation more cost-effective. Transportation managers need to stay informed about trade agreements to capitalize on cost-saving opportunities.

8.4 Liability and Insurance Considerations

Managing liability and insurance is essential in transportation to protect companies from financial loss and ensure compliance with regulations.

8.4.1 Types of Liability in Transportation

Carrier Liability: Carriers are responsible for the goods they transport and may be held liable if cargo is damaged or lost. Carrier liability is generally limited by law, and companies often secure additional insurance to cover the value of the cargo.

Third-Party Liability: Transportation providers may also be liable for damages or injuries to third parties, such as accidents involving other vehicles or individuals. Liability coverage is necessary to mitigate the financial impact of these incidents.

8.4.2 Insurance Options for Transportation

Cargo Insurance: Cargo insurance covers the goods in transit, providing protection against loss, theft, or damage. Coverage levels vary, and companies can opt for either "all-risk" or "named perils" policies depending on the level of risk they are willing to accept.

Liability Insurance: Liability insurance protects transportation providers against claims arising from accidents, injuries, or damage to third parties. Comprehensive liability insurance helps reduce financial exposure in case of unforeseen incidents.

Errors and Omissions Insurance: Errors and omissions (E&O) insurance protects logistics providers from claims resulting from unintentional errors in documentation, customs procedures, or other operational aspects.

8.4.3 Best Practices for Managing Liability and Insurance

Conduct Risk Assessments: Regular risk assessments help identify potential liability issues, allowing companies to address them proactively through appropriate insurance and safety measures.

Regularly Review Insurance Coverage: Transportation managers should review insurance policies periodically to ensure adequate coverage as the business grows and risks evolve.

Use Technology for Documentation Accuracy: Accurate and thorough documentation is essential to avoid liability issues. Transportation management systems (TMS) and automated documentation tools can help reduce errors and improve compliance.

Legal and regulatory considerations are critical aspects of transportation management that directly affect operational efficiency, cost, and compliance. By understanding the fundamental laws governing transportation, businesses can avoid legal issues and build a more resilient supply chain. Compliance with customs regulations, careful management of tariffs and duties, and comprehensive liability coverage contribute to successful cross-border operations and reduce the likelihood of costly disruptions. With the dynamic regulatory environment, companies must remain vigilant, adapting their practices to changing laws and leveraging technology to streamline compliance processes. Through proactive legal and regulatory management, companies can ensure the safe and efficient movement of goods while minimizing risks and upholding ethical standards in their transportation operations.

This chapter provides a structured view of the legal considerations within transportation management, helping businesses navigate complexities and build a compliant, resilient transportation strategy.

Chapter 9: Technology in Transportation Management

Transportation Management Systems (TMS) Overview

Role of GPS, IoT, and Blockchain in Tracking and Security

Use of Data Analytics and AI in Transportation

Future Trends in Transportation Technology

Technology has revolutionized transportation management, transforming how companies plan, execute, and monitor their logistics operations. With innovations like Transportation Management Systems (TMS), GPS, IoT, blockchain, data analytics, and artificial intelligence (AI), businesses can now achieve unprecedented levels of efficiency, visibility, and security in their transportation processes. This chapter explores the role of key technologies in transportation management, their applications, and the future trends shaping the industry.

9.1 Transportation Management Systems (TMS) Overview

A Transportation Management System (TMS) is software that helps businesses manage and streamline their transportation operations. TMS platforms allow companies to automate processes, improve routing, reduce costs, and enhance customer satisfaction.

9.1.1 Functions and Benefits of TMS

Route Planning and Optimization: TMS solutions can suggest optimal routes based on distance, fuel consumption, and delivery timelines. This helps minimize travel time and costs.

Carrier Selection and Management: TMS software aids in selecting carriers based on cost, availability, and reliability, ensuring the best-fit choice for each shipment. It also supports carrier performance tracking.

Load Optimization: TMS can maximize space utilization by consolidating shipments, thereby reducing transportation costs and carbon footprint.

Real-Time Tracking and Visibility: Real-time tracking is crucial for businesses to monitor shipment status and proactively address delays or issues. TMS solutions offer live data, keeping all stakeholders informed.

Cost Control and Freight Auditing: TMS platforms track transportation expenses and conduct freight audits to detect and correct billing discrepancies. Cost analytics provided by TMS can guide budgeting and cost reduction strategies.

Enhanced Customer Service: By providing accurate ETAs, tracking information, and on-time delivery, TMS enhances customer satisfaction and transparency.

9.1.2 Challenges and Considerations in TMS Implementation

While TMS offers numerous advantages, implementing such systems requires careful planning. Common challenges include high upfront costs, training requirements, data integration with existing ERP (Enterprise Resource Planning) systems, and data accuracy. Companies must ensure that their TMS solution integrates seamlessly with their broader IT infrastructure and addresses specific business needs.

9.2 Role of GPS, IoT, and Blockchain in Tracking and Security

Emerging technologies such as GPS, the Internet of Things (IoT), and blockchain have greatly enhanced tracking and security in transportation management, offering companies new ways to secure and monitor their shipments in real time.

9.2.1 GPS for Real-Time Location Tracking

GPS (Global Positioning System) technology provides precise location data for vehicles, shipments, and fleets, helping businesses track deliveries and monitor vehicle movements. This improves route efficiency, helps identify delays, and enables accurate ETA (Estimated Time of Arrival) predictions. GPS data also supports geofencing, where alerts are triggered if a vehicle deviates from its designated route, enhancing security for high-value cargo.

9.2.2 IoT in Transportation Management

IoT uses sensors to gather real-time data on the condition and location of goods, vehicles, and assets. In transportation management, IoT enables:

Cargo Condition Monitoring: IoT sensors can monitor cargo conditions such as temperature, humidity, and shock, crucial for sensitive goods like food, pharmaceuticals, and electronics.

If conditions deviate from acceptable levels, alerts are triggered to prevent spoilage or damage.

Vehicle Performance and Maintenance: IoT devices track vehicle performance metrics, including fuel consumption, tire pressure, and engine health. By monitoring these factors, companies can anticipate maintenance needs, avoid breakdowns, and improve fleet reliability.

Enhanced Security: IoT technology can improve security through real-time tracking of trailers, cargo containers, and even individual pallets. Anti-theft systems, powered by IoT, alert managers if there is unauthorized access or tampering.

9.2.3 Blockchain for Secure Data Sharing

Blockchain is a decentralized and secure ledger technology that allows transparent and tamper-proof data sharing among stakeholders. In transportation management, blockchain supports:

Secure Data Exchange: Blockchain ensures that all parties, including shippers, carriers, and customs officials, have access to a shared, secure data record. This reduces discrepancies and increases accountability.

Enhanced Documentation and Compliance: Blockchain can automate document processing, allowing for seamless, tamper-proof transfer of documentation like bills of lading, certificates, and invoices. This enhances regulatory compliance and reduces delays.

Fraud Prevention and Transparency: Blockchain's immutability prevents fraud, ensuring all transactions and data entries remain unaltered. This transparency builds trust among stakeholders and reduces disputes in international shipping.

9.3 Use of Data Analytics and AI in Transportation

Data analytics and artificial intelligence (AI) play a vital role in optimizing transportation management, allowing companies to make informed, data-driven decisions.

9.3.1 Data Analytics in Transportation

Data analytics involves examining data to extract insights that can improve operational efficiency and decision-making. Applications of data analytics in transportation include:

Demand Forecasting: Analyzing historical shipment data allows businesses to predict demand accurately, plan resources, and optimize fleet deployment.

Cost Analysis: Detailed analysis of transportation costs by lane, mode, and carrier enables companies to identify high-cost areas and implement cost-saving measures.

Performance Monitoring: Data analytics helps track key performance indicators (KPIs) like on-time delivery rates, transit times, and fuel efficiency, allowing managers to monitor and improve performance.

9.3.2 Artificial Intelligence (AI) Applications in Transportation

AI enables predictive analytics, automation, and intelligent decision-making in transportation management. Key AI applications include:

Predictive Maintenance: By analyzing vehicle data, AI can predict maintenance needs, allowing companies to conduct timely repairs and prevent breakdowns.

Route Optimization and Dynamic Routing: AI-powered algorithms assess variables such as traffic, weather, and fuel costs to suggest the most efficient routes. Dynamic routing, enabled by AI, adjusts routes in real-time based on changing conditions.

Automated Freight Matching: AI can automatically match shipments with carriers based on factors like cost, capacity, and destination, improving asset utilization and reducing empty miles.

Autonomous Vehicles and Robotics: While still in the early stages, AI-driven autonomous vehicles and robotic systems are set to transform last-mile delivery, warehouse automation, and fleet operations.

9.4 Future Trends in Transportation Technology

Technological advances are continuously reshaping the transportation industry. Anticipating and adapting to these trends is essential for maintaining competitive advantage.

9.4.1 Autonomous Vehicles

Autonomous vehicles, including trucks and drones, have the potential to revolutionize logistics by reducing reliance on human drivers and increasing delivery speed. Although regulatory and safety concerns must be addressed, self-driving trucks and drones could become a viable option for last-mile delivery and regional transport.

9.4.2 Electric Vehicles and Sustainability

The transportation industry is under growing pressure to reduce carbon emissions. Electric vehicles (EVs) offer a sustainable alternative, with companies like Tesla, Volvo, and Daimler investing in electric trucks. As EV charging infrastructure expands, electric vehicles will become more practical for long-haul transportation, lowering the environmental impact.

9.4.3 Hyperloop and High-Speed Rail

Innovative transport methods like the hyperloop and high-speed rail could redefine the future of freight transportation. The hyperloop, a proposed high-speed transport system, aims to reduce transit times drastically by moving goods at speeds of up to 700 miles per hour. Although still in the conceptual stage, these technologies offer potential solutions for faster, more sustainable freight movement.

9.4.4 Artificial Intelligence and Machine Learning for Proactive Management

AI and machine learning will continue to evolve, enabling more proactive and predictive management of transportation networks. From anticipating weather-related disruptions to optimizing cargo space, machine learning algorithms will offer advanced solutions that adapt to real-time data and changing market dynamics.

9.4.5 Advanced Telematics and IoT Integration

IoT and telematics will become increasingly interconnected, allowing transportation managers to access a continuous stream of data on vehicle conditions, traffic patterns, and cargo status. Enhanced IoT integration will lead to better fleet management, improved fuel efficiency, and proactive maintenance.

Technology is transforming every aspect of transportation management, from real-time tracking to data-driven decision-making and automation. TMS, GPS, IoT, blockchain, data analytics, and AI are now essential components of a modern transportation strategy, providing the tools needed to optimize costs, improve customer service, and ensure secure and compliant operations. Looking forward, trends like autonomous vehicles, electric trucks, and hyperloop technology are set to further revolutionize the industry, driving the next wave of efficiency, sustainability, and innovation. By staying informed and adapting to these technological advancements, transportation managers can better prepare for the future and maintain a competitive edge in an ever-evolving landscape.

Chapter 10: Sustainability in Transportation

Environmental Impact of Transportation

Green Transportation Initiatives

Reducing Carbon Emissions and Energy Consumption

Case Studies on Sustainable Transportation Practices

Sustainability is increasingly a core focus in transportation management as environmental impact concerns shape corporate strategies and regulatory standards. The transportation sector is a significant contributor to greenhouse gas emissions, air pollution, and energy consumption, making sustainable practices critical. This chapter explores the environmental impacts of transportation, green transportation initiatives, methods to reduce emissions and energy consumption, and case studies highlighting sustainable practices.

10.1 Environmental Impact of Transportation

The transportation sector has a significant environmental footprint, affecting both ecosystems and human health. Key impacts include:

Greenhouse Gas Emissions: Transportation is one of the largest sources of greenhouse gas (GHG) emissions globally, primarily due to the combustion of fossil fuels. Carbon dioxide (CO_2) is the most prevalent GHG emitted, followed by methane (CH_4) and nitrous oxide (N_2O).

Air Pollution: Besides GHGs, transportation contributes to pollutants like sulfur dioxide (SO_2), nitrogen oxides (NO_x), carbon monoxide (CO), and particulate matter (PM). These pollutants are harmful to respiratory health and contribute to acid rain and smog.

Energy Consumption: Transportation relies heavily on non-renewable energy sources, such as gasoline and diesel, which not only deplete finite resources but also contribute to pollution.

Habitat Disruption: Infrastructure projects like highways, railroads, and ports often disrupt natural habitats, impacting biodiversity. Urban sprawl and road construction can fragment wildlife habitats, causing species displacement and threatening ecosystems.

Water and Soil Pollution: Transportation can lead to oil spills, chemical leaks, and other hazardous discharges that affect soil and water quality. Road runoff can introduce pollutants into water bodies, affecting aquatic life and drinking water sources.

10.2 Green Transportation Initiatives

Green transportation initiatives aim to reduce the negative environmental impact of transportation through sustainable practices, policies, and technologies. Key initiatives include:

10.2.1 Sustainable Fuel Alternatives

Switching to sustainable fuel sources, such as biodiesel, ethanol, hydrogen, and electricity, is a major focus in green transportation. Electric vehicles (EVs) are a leading solution, with companies investing in EV fleets to cut emissions. Hydrogen fuel cells and biofuels are also promising alternatives, offering reduced carbon emissions for long-haul and heavy-duty vehicles.

10.2.2 Eco-Friendly Logistics Planning

Logistics planning can be optimized to minimize fuel consumption and emissions. Green logistics practices include optimizing routes, consolidating shipments, and reducing empty miles. Technologies like telematics, which provides real-time data on fuel usage, driver behavior, and vehicle health, help companies make data-driven decisions for sustainable logistics.

10.2.3 Carbon Offsetting Programs

Some companies offset their emissions through carbon offsetting programs, which invest in projects like reforestation, renewable energy, and methane capture to compensate for the carbon emitted by transportation activities. Carbon offsets are especially useful for companies that cannot eliminate emissions entirely but want to mitigate their environmental impact.

10.2.4 Green Supply Chain Partnerships

Collaboration with green-conscious suppliers and carriers is another effective way to promote sustainability. Companies are increasingly setting sustainability criteria for their suppliers and partners, encouraging a collective move towards environmentally friendly practices. By prioritizing partnerships with green-certified suppliers, companies can reduce emissions across their supply chains.

10.2.5 Urban and Regional Initiatives

Local governments and businesses are working together to create sustainable urban transportation systems. Examples include implementing low-emission zones, promoting electric buses and rail systems, developing bike-sharing programs, and expanding charging infrastructure for EVs. These initiatives help cities reduce emissions, traffic congestion, and pollution levels.

10.3 Reducing Carbon Emissions and Energy Consumption

Reducing emissions and energy use in transportation requires a combination of technology, policy, and behavioral change. Strategies for achieving these goals include:

10.3.1 Fleet Electrification

Switching to electric vehicles is one of the most effective ways to reduce carbon emissions. Although electric trucks and commercial vehicles are still emerging, companies are investing in electrification as battery technology improves and EV infrastructure expands. Electric fleets emit zero tailpipe emissions, making them ideal for urban deliveries and short-distance travel.

10.3.2 Fuel Efficiency Optimization

For companies unable to transition to electric fleets, optimizing fuel efficiency is a valuable approach to reducing emissions. Techniques to improve fuel efficiency include:

Eco-Driving Practices: Training drivers in eco-driving techniques, such as avoiding sudden accelerations and braking, can reduce fuel consumption.

Aerodynamic Design: Vehicles with improved aerodynamics require less fuel to overcome air resistance, which can lower fuel costs and emissions.

Weight Reduction: Reducing vehicle weight through lightweight materials or load optimization can improve fuel economy and reduce emissions.

10.3.3 Alternative Fuels

Alternative fuels like compressed natural gas (CNG), liquefied natural gas (LNG), and biofuels are becoming popular for reducing carbon emissions. Biofuels, derived from organic materials like vegetable oil or animal fats, emit fewer pollutants than traditional fossil fuels and can be a feasible option for long-haul trucks and ships.

10.3.4 Renewable Energy for Logistics Facilities

Companies are increasingly powering warehouses, distribution centers, and offices with renewable energy sources such as solar and wind. This reduces their overall carbon footprint and supports sustainability goals. Additionally, renewable-powered facilities contribute to a greener supply chain, especially when combined with energy-efficient lighting, heating, and cooling systems.

10.3.5 Reducing Empty Miles and Load Optimization

Transportation companies can reduce emissions and costs by minimizing empty miles (the distance traveled without cargo) and optimizing load capacities. Implementing TMS and load-matching technologies can improve vehicle utilization, while sharing resources through collaborative transportation networks can enhance efficiency.

10.3.6 Mode Shifting

Choosing the right mode of transport can reduce emissions and energy usage. For instance, rail and water transport generally produce lower emissions per ton-mile compared to road and air freight. Mode shifting—transitioning from air or road to rail or maritime where possible—can be a strategic way to improve sustainability.

10.4 Case Studies on Sustainable Transportation Practices

Real-world examples of companies implementing sustainable transportation practices illustrate the effectiveness of these initiatives.

10.4.1 UPS: Route Optimization and Carbon Neutrality Goals

UPS has implemented a sophisticated route optimization system, ORION (On-Road Integrated Optimization and Navigation), which has reduced millions of miles driven annually by creating efficient delivery routes. This system factors in variables such as traffic, package volume, and customer requirements, minimizing fuel use and emissions. UPS has also committed to achieving carbon neutrality by 2050, using a combination of EV adoption, fuel-efficient vehicles, and renewable energy.

10.4.2 Tesla's Electric Freight Vehicles

Tesla's electric trucks, the Tesla Semi, are designed to lower carbon emissions for long-haul freight transport. Tesla claims that the Semi will reduce fuel costs by up to 20% compared to diesel trucks, while its all-electric design cuts tailpipe emissions entirely. Though still in its early stages, Tesla's model is driving the adoption of electric heavy-duty vehicles, setting a benchmark for sustainable freight solutions.

10.4.3 DHL's GoGreen Program

DHL, a global logistics provider, has set ambitious goals to reduce its carbon footprint through its GoGreen program. The company's initiatives include using alternative fuels, enhancing fleet efficiency, and developing green warehouses powered by renewable energy. DHL has also implemented a carbon-neutral shipping service, offering clients the opportunity to offset emissions associated with their shipments.

10.4.4 IKEA's Commitment to Zero Emissions Deliveries

IKEA has pledged to make all of its last-mile deliveries zero emissions by 2025, focusing on urban areas where pollution and congestion are most prevalent. The company is investing in electric delivery vans and working closely with delivery partners to achieve this goal. IKEA's commitment to zero emissions delivery aligns with its larger sustainability strategy, which includes reducing its overall carbon footprint and promoting circular business practices.

10.4.5 Maersk's Carbon-Neutral Shipping Goals

Maersk, a leader in maritime logistics, is pioneering sustainable practices in ocean freight by investing in biofuels and targeting a carbon-neutral fleet by 2050. The company is exploring alternative fuels such as green ammonia and methanol, as well as energy-efficient vessel designs. Maersk's commitment to carbon neutrality positions it as a sustainability leader in global shipping.

Sustainability in transportation management is both a responsibility and a strategic advantage for businesses. By adopting green transportation initiatives, investing in sustainable technologies, and optimizing logistics processes, companies can reduce their environmental impact while maintaining operational efficiency. As demonstrated in the case studies, leading organizations are already achieving measurable benefits through their sustainability efforts. In the future, regulatory pressures, consumer demand, and technological advances will continue to drive the adoption of sustainable practices in transportation, making it essential for companies to prioritize environmental stewardship as part of their long-term strategies.

Chapter 11: Performance Measurement in Transportation

Key Performance Indicators (KPIs) for Transportation

Measuring Efficiency, Cost, and Customer Satisfaction

Tools for Performance Monitoring and Reporting

Continuous Improvement in Transportation Management

Performance measurement is critical in transportation management, as it helps organizations assess the efficiency, effectiveness, and cost-effectiveness of their transportation operations. By tracking key performance indicators (KPIs), transportation managers can gain insights into areas of improvement, identify trends, and ensure alignment with organizational goals. This chapter explores the KPIs that are essential for evaluating transportation performance, tools for monitoring and reporting, and strategies for fostering continuous improvement in transportation management.

11.1 Key Performance Indicators (KPIs) for Transportation

Key Performance Indicators (KPIs) are metrics that help organizations measure the success of their transportation operations. These indicators provide a quantifiable means to evaluate performance against set objectives, benchmark against industry standards, and identify opportunities for improvement. Some of the most important KPIs for transportation management include:

11.1.1 On-Time Delivery (OTD)

On-time delivery is a critical metric for customer satisfaction. It measures the percentage of shipments delivered by the promised time. A high OTD rate reflects efficient scheduling, effective route planning, and strong carrier performance. Low OTD rates may indicate issues with route optimization, delays in loading or unloading, or poor supplier performance.

Formula:

OTD

$$OTD = \left(\frac{\text{Number of On-Time Deliveries}}{\text{Total Number of Deliveries}} \right) \times 100$$

11.1.2 Transportation Costs per Unit or Shipment

This KPI measures the cost incurred for transporting goods, either by unit, weight, or per shipment. It helps assess the efficiency of cost management in transportation and identifies trends that may signal areas for cost optimization, such as carrier rate negotiations, fuel usage, or vehicle maintenance.

Formula:

$$\text{Cost per Shipment} = \frac{\text{Total Transportation Costs}}{\text{Total Number of Shipments}}$$

11.1.3 Fuel Efficiency

Fuel efficiency is a vital KPI for reducing transportation costs and minimizing environmental impact. It measures the amount of fuel consumed per distance traveled or per unit of cargo. Improving fuel efficiency contributes directly to cost reduction and supports sustainability efforts.

Formula:

$$\text{Fuel Efficiency} = \frac{\text{Total Distance Traveled}}{\text{Total Fuel Consumed}}$$

11.1.4 Damage or Claims Rate

This KPI tracks the percentage of shipments that are damaged or result in claims. A high rate of damage often indicates issues in packaging, handling, or transportation conditions. Reducing this metric requires improvements in these areas to enhance product protection and reduce insurance claims.

Formula:

$$\text{Damage Rate} = \left(\frac{\text{Number of Damaged Shipments}}{\text{Total Shipments}} \right) \times 100$$

11.1.5 Carrier Performance

This KPI evaluates the performance of third-party carriers based on delivery reliability, timeliness, and quality of service. By regularly assessing carrier performance, transportation managers can make informed decisions about which carriers to continue working with and where improvements are needed.

11.1.6 Transportation Time (Lead Time)

Transportation lead time measures the total time taken from when an order is placed until it is delivered. Reducing transportation lead time enhances customer satisfaction by providing faster service. This KPI is especially important in industries like e-commerce, where quick delivery is a key competitive advantage.

Lead Time=Time of Delivery−Time of Shipment

11.1.7 Empty Miles (Deadhead Miles)

Empty miles refer to the distance traveled by vehicles without carrying cargo. This metric is crucial for reducing fuel consumption and improving fleet efficiency. Minimizing empty miles is an important strategy for cost reduction and environmental sustainability.

Formula:

$$\text{Empty Miles} = \left(\frac{\text{Empty Miles Traveled}}{\text{Total Miles Traveled}} \right) \times 100$$

11.1.8 Customer Satisfaction

Customer satisfaction can be measured through surveys, feedback forms, and performance metrics such as complaint rates and returns. It evaluates how well transportation services meet customer expectations regarding speed, reliability, cost, and communication.

11.2 Measuring Efficiency, Cost, and Customer Satisfaction

Effectively measuring transportation performance involves a comprehensive assessment of efficiency, cost, and customer satisfaction. Here's how organizations can evaluate these critical aspects:

11.2.1 Measuring Efficiency

Efficiency in transportation refers to how well resources (e.g., time, vehicles, labor) are utilized to achieve transportation objectives. To measure efficiency, companies use the following metrics:

Utilization Rates: Measures how effectively assets like trucks, trailers, and warehouse space are utilized.

Average Speed/Travel Time: Assesses how fast goods are transported from origin to destination, factoring in delays, stops, and route optimization.

Route Efficiency: Examines how well optimized transportation routes are, considering fuel consumption, time, and distance.

11.2.2 Measuring Cost

Transportation costs are a major consideration for businesses aiming to remain competitive. Companies measure transportation cost through several dimensions:

Cost Per Mile: Measures the cost incurred for every mile traveled by a vehicle, taking into account fuel, maintenance, and driver wages.

Cost Per Unit Shipped: Assesses the cost for each item or unit shipped, factoring in all expenses such as packaging, labor, and transportation fees.

Fixed vs. Variable Costs: Understanding fixed (e.g., truck payments, insurance) and variable (e.g., fuel, tolls) costs helps businesses plan for both predictable and fluctuating expenses.

11.2.3 Measuring Customer Satisfaction

Customer satisfaction in transportation management can be influenced by many factors, including delivery timeliness, quality of service, and communication. To measure satisfaction, organizations can use:

Net Promoter Score (NPS): A common metric that gauges customer loyalty and satisfaction based on whether customers would recommend the service to others.

Customer Feedback: Direct input from customers can provide valuable insights into areas such as service quality, delivery speed, and packaging conditions.

Complaint Tracking: Monitoring the frequency and nature of customer complaints helps identify areas that need improvement in the transportation process.

11.3 Tools for Performance Monitoring and Reporting

Transportation performance management relies on several tools and technologies to track, monitor, and report KPIs. These tools help transportation managers make data-driven decisions to improve operational efficiency and customer service.

11.3.1 Transportation Management Systems (TMS)

A TMS is the backbone of performance monitoring in transportation. It provides real-time data on shipment status, route optimization, carrier performance, and cost analysis. By integrating a TMS with other enterprise systems like Enterprise Resource Planning (ERP), businesses can gain insights across the entire supply chain.

11.3.2 Fleet Management Software

Fleet management software helps track fleet performance by providing data on vehicle location, fuel usage, maintenance schedules, and driver behavior. These insights enable managers to optimize fleet performance, reduce fuel consumption, and ensure timely maintenance.

11.3.3 GPS and Telematics Systems

GPS tracking and telematics systems provide real-time visibility into vehicle locations and movement. They allow transportation managers to monitor factors like speed, idling time, and route deviations, which can be used to improve efficiency and reduce delays.

11.3.4 Business Intelligence (BI) Tools

BI tools provide comprehensive reporting and analysis capabilities. With BI software, transportation managers can create custom dashboards to visualize performance data, identify trends, and compare performance over time. This enables more strategic decision-making based on data-driven insights.

11.3.5 Performance Dashboards

Real-time performance dashboards are essential for continuous monitoring. These dashboards display real-time data on key KPIs such as on-time delivery, fuel efficiency, and transportation costs. With customized alerts and notifications, managers can quickly address issues as they arise.

11.4 Continuous Improvement in Transportation Management

To stay competitive and reduce operational inefficiencies, transportation management requires a continuous improvement mindset. This involves using feedback and data to make incremental adjustments and drive long-term improvements.

11.4.1 Lean Transportation Management

Lean principles, such as eliminating waste and optimizing processes, can be applied to transportation. For example, reducing empty miles, optimizing warehouse layout, and improving loading/unloading times are all lean practices that lead to better utilization of resources and lower transportation costs.

11.4.2 Kaizen

Kaizen, the Japanese practice of continuous, incremental improvement, can be applied to transportation management by encouraging employees at all levels to contribute ideas for improving processes. Small changes over time, such as improving route planning, enhancing communication with customers, or reducing vehicle downtime, can result in significant long-term benefits.

11.4.3 Performance Reviews and Benchmarking

Regular performance reviews and benchmarking against industry standards or competitors help identify areas where performance can be improved. Companies can use KPIs and best practices from other organizations as a guide to achieving operational excellence.

11.4.4 Employee Training and Development

Ongoing training is essential for keeping transportation teams updated on best practices, new technologies, and regulations. Training programs focusing on safety, fuel efficiency, customer service, and route optimization can contribute to continuous improvement in transportation performance.

Effective performance measurement is key to ensuring that transportation operations are efficient, cost-effective, and aligned with customer expectations. By focusing on critical KPIs such as on-time delivery, cost efficiency, and customer satisfaction, transportation managers can monitor performance, identify areas for improvement, and make data-driven decisions. With the right tools for monitoring and reporting, along with a commitment to continuous improvement, businesses can

Chapter 12: Collaboration and Third-Party Logistics (3PL)

Benefits and Challenges of Outsourcing Transportation

Selecting and Managing 3PL Partners

Collaboration with Suppliers and Customers

Case Studies on Effective 3PL Relationships

In today's complex supply chain environment, many companies are opting to collaborate with third-party logistics providers (3PLs) to enhance their transportation operations. Outsourcing transportation functions to 3PL partners allows organizations to leverage expertise, resources, and technology, while focusing on their core competencies. This chapter examines the benefits and challenges of outsourcing transportation to 3PLs, how to select and manage 3PL partners, and the importance of collaboration with suppliers and customers to optimize transportation processes.

12.1 Benefits and Challenges of Outsourcing Transportation

Outsourcing transportation to third-party logistics providers offers several benefits, but it also presents challenges that must be carefully managed. Understanding these pros and cons is crucial for companies considering 3PL partnerships.

12.1.1 Benefits of Outsourcing Transportation

Cost Efficiency

One of the most significant advantages of using a 3PL is the potential for cost savings. 3PLs have established networks, scale, and expertise, allowing them to negotiate better rates with carriers, optimize routes, and improve overall transportation efficiency. By outsourcing transportation, companies can reduce overhead costs related to fleet management, labor, and vehicle maintenance.

Access to Advanced Technology

3PL providers often invest in cutting-edge technology, such as Transportation Management Systems (TMS), GPS tracking, and real-time monitoring, which can enhance transportation visibility, optimize routes, and provide data analytics for better decision-making. Small and medium-sized businesses that cannot afford to invest in these technologies themselves can gain access to them by partnering with 3PLs.

Scalability and Flexibility

Using a 3PL enables companies to scale their transportation operations up or down depending on business needs. This flexibility is particularly important for businesses with fluctuating demands or seasonal variations. Whether shipping more goods during peak seasons or scaling back during low-demand periods, 3PLs can adjust capacity and resources quickly to meet changing needs.

Expertise and Focus

Transportation management requires significant expertise, including knowledge of regulations, compliance standards, and best practices. By outsourcing to a 3PL, companies can tap into this specialized knowledge. This allows the internal team to focus on strategic activities while leaving the operational details to experts in logistics.

Improved Service Levels

3PLs, with their extensive experience in transportation, can often offer higher levels of service, such as better on-time delivery rates, real-time tracking, and customer support. They are also well-versed in handling issues like customs and tariffs, providing smoother cross-border transportation.

12.1.2 Challenges of Outsourcing Transportation

Loss of Control

One of the primary concerns when outsourcing transportation is the potential loss of control over day-to-day operations. Companies may be less involved in decisions regarding route optimization, carrier selection, and customer communication. This loss of control can impact customer experience and service quality if not managed properly.

Dependence on Third Parties

Outsourcing creates a reliance on third-party providers, which means any issues with the 3PL—such as operational inefficiencies, delays, or miscommunications—can directly affect the business. If a 3PL fails to meet expectations, the company may face significant operational disruptions, customer dissatisfaction, and brand reputation damage.

Hidden Costs

While 3PL partnerships can offer cost savings, there can be hidden costs, such as additional fees for storage, special handling, or last-minute changes in service requirements. Companies must be diligent in understanding the full scope of fees associated with 3PL services to avoid unexpected expenses.

Cultural and Communication Barriers

In global 3PL partnerships, language barriers, cultural differences, and time zone challenges can make effective communication difficult. These barriers can lead to misunderstandings, errors in shipments, and delays, all of which affect performance and customer satisfaction.

Vendor Reliability

Choosing an unreliable 3PL can have far-reaching consequences. It is important to select partners with a proven track record in transportation reliability, regulatory compliance, and customer service. Failing to do so can result in delays, damages, and potential legal issues.

12.2 Selecting and Managing 3PL Partners

The selection of a reliable and effective 3PL partner is crucial to the success of outsourcing transportation. The right partner can help optimize transportation, improve service levels, and drive cost efficiencies. Conversely, choosing the wrong 3PL can result in operational disruptions and damage to customer relationships.

12.2.1 Key Considerations When Selecting a 3PL Partner

Experience and Expertise

The 3PL's experience in the industry, its knowledge of transportation regulations, and its ability to handle specific types of cargo are important factors to consider. A 3PL with a proven track record in the relevant market (e.g., perishable goods, high-value products, or international shipping) will likely be more successful at meeting the specific needs of the business.

Technology Capabilities

As technology plays an increasingly critical role in transportation management, it is important to assess the 3PL's technology infrastructure. A 3PL should offer a robust Transportation Management System (TMS), real-time tracking, GPS monitoring, and analytics to improve visibility, enhance efficiency, and reduce errors.

Financial Stability

The financial health of the 3PL provider is another important consideration. Financial stability ensures that the provider has the resources necessary to maintain operations, invest in technology, and scale as needed. A financially unstable 3PL can create risks for the business in terms of service interruptions or price hikes.

Geographical Reach and Network

The 3PL's geographic reach and transportation network must align with the business's supply chain requirements. A global 3PL provider with a wide-reaching network can help businesses expand their reach into new markets, while a regional 3PL may offer more specialized services.

Customer Service and Communication

Excellent customer service and effective communication are vital in any 3PL relationship. The provider should have responsive customer support, easy-to-use communication channels, and the ability to handle issues quickly and efficiently. Companies should also look for partners who offer regular performance reports, allowing them to track service levels and identify areas for improvement.

12.2.2 Managing 3PL Relationships

Clear Service Level Agreements (SLAs)

Establishing clear SLAs with 3PL providers is crucial to ensuring both parties understand their responsibilities and expectations. SLAs should specify performance metrics such as on-time delivery, handling procedures, and cost structures. Regular performance reviews should be conducted to assess the 3PL's adherence to these SLAs.

Regular Communication and Collaboration

Maintaining regular communication with the 3PL partner helps address any potential issues before they escalate. Collaborative meetings and check-ins can provide updates on performance, discuss potential challenges, and identify opportunities for improvement.

Data Sharing and Transparency

Transparency in data sharing can improve trust and efficiency. Companies and their 3PL partners should exchange real-time data on inventory levels, shipments, and any changes in demand. This open flow of information ensures that both parties can respond proactively to issues.

Continuous Improvement

A partnership with a 3PL should be seen as a long-term collaboration. Continuous improvement efforts, such as jointly working on process optimization, exploring new technologies, and finding ways to reduce costs, can benefit both parties. A mutually beneficial partnership leads to greater value over time.

12.3 Collaboration with Suppliers and Customers

Effective collaboration with both suppliers and customers is key to optimizing transportation and ensuring smooth supply chain operations. This section explores how collaboration with these stakeholders enhances transportation management.

12.3.1 Collaboration with Suppliers

Suppliers play a crucial role in the transportation process, as their performance impacts delivery times, packaging, and inventory management. Collaborative relationships with suppliers can improve transportation efficiency in the following ways:

Joint Planning: Working with suppliers to forecast demand and plan shipments reduces the risk of overstocking or understocking.

Packaging Optimization: Collaboration on packaging can minimize damage during transit and improve loading efficiency.

Inventory Visibility: Sharing inventory data allows for better coordination of shipments, leading to fewer delays and optimized warehouse operations.

12.3.2 Collaboration with Customers

Customer collaboration is essential for understanding delivery expectations and improving service levels. Effective customer relationships contribute to transportation success in the following ways:

Demand Forecasting: Collaborating on demand forecasting helps align transportation capacity with expected demand, reducing stockouts or overstocking.

Flexible Delivery Options: Offering customers multiple delivery options, such as time-sensitive or cost-effective shipping, can enhance satisfaction while reducing transportation costs.

Feedback Loops: Regular feedback from customers helps identify areas for improvement in transportation and allows businesses to make adjustments to improve service quality.

12.4 Case Studies on Effective 3PL Relationships

Case Study 1: A Global Consumer Goods Company

A global consumer goods company partnered with a 3PL provider to streamline its transportation operations across multiple continents. The company leveraged the 3PL's established network and expertise in managing international shipping, ensuring timely deliveries and reducing transportation costs. By sharing data with the 3PL and working collaboratively on route optimization, the company was able to reduce lead times by 10% and transportation costs by 15% within the first year of the partnership.

Case Study 2: E-Commerce Retailer

An e-commerce retailer partnered with a regional 3PL provider to handle last-mile delivery and improve customer service levels. By working closely with the 3PL to offer flexible delivery options and improve communication channels with customers, the retailer achieved a 20% improvement in on-time deliveries and significantly enhanced customer satisfaction.

Collaboration with third-party

logistics providers, suppliers, and customers can significantly enhance transportation operations, improve efficiency, and drive cost savings. By carefully selecting 3PL partners, managing these relationships effectively, and fostering collaboration across the supply chain, businesses can overcome challenges and maximize the benefits of outsourcing transportation.

12.5 Building Strong Collaborative Relationships

Developing robust collaborative relationships with 3PL providers, suppliers, and customers requires ongoing effort, strategic alignment, and clear communication. This section outlines practical steps to strengthen these relationships for long-term success.

12.5.1 Strategic Alignment

Collaboration is most effective when all parties share aligned goals and priorities. Businesses should work with their 3PL providers and supply chain partners to establish mutual objectives, such as reducing lead times, minimizing costs, or enhancing customer satisfaction. Strategic alignment ensures that all stakeholders are working towards the same outcomes, fostering a spirit of cooperation and partnership.

12.5.2 Shared Data and Technology Platforms

The adoption of shared data platforms and technologies can enhance collaboration by providing real-time visibility into transportation activities. Collaborative tools like cloud-based Transportation Management Systems (TMS) and integrated dashboards enable seamless information sharing between companies, 3PLs, and other stakeholders. These tools help ensure that everyone has access to the same data, facilitating better decision-making and quicker responses to transportation challenges.

12.5.3 Performance Metrics and Accountability

Establishing clear metrics and accountability frameworks is essential for successful collaboration. Businesses should develop Key Performance Indicators (KPIs) to measure the performance of their 3PL providers and supply chain partners. Regular reviews and feedback sessions allow for continuous monitoring and improvement. Transparent reporting ensures that all parties remain accountable for their roles in achieving transportation objectives.

12.5.4 Trust and Long-Term Relationships

Building trust is the foundation of successful collaboration. Companies should focus on developing long-term partnerships rather than transactional relationships with their 3PLs and other partners. This involves open communication, a willingness to share risks and rewards, and demonstrating reliability over time. Trust fosters greater cooperation and a commitment to mutual success.

12.6 Innovations in Third-Party Logistics

The field of third-party logistics is rapidly evolving, driven by technological advancements and changing market dynamics. Innovations in 3PL services are creating new opportunities for businesses to enhance their transportation strategies.

12.6.1 Automation and Robotics

Many 3PL providers are incorporating automation and robotics into their operations, particularly in warehouses and distribution centers. Automated systems can sort, pack, and load goods more quickly and accurately than human labor, reducing errors and speeding up transportation processes.

12.6.2 Predictive Analytics

Predictive analytics is transforming how 3PL providers plan and execute transportation activities. By analyzing historical data and real-time information, predictive tools can forecast demand, identify potential risks, and recommend optimal shipping routes. These insights help businesses stay ahead of challenges and make data-driven decisions.

12.6.3 Sustainability Initiatives

Sustainability is becoming a key focus for 3PL providers. Many are adopting eco-friendly practices, such as using electric or hybrid vehicles, optimizing delivery routes to reduce fuel consumption, and implementing sustainable packaging solutions. These initiatives help businesses meet environmental goals while enhancing their brand reputation.

12.6.4 Blockchain Technology

Blockchain technology is being used by some 3PL providers to improve transparency and security in the transportation process. Blockchain creates an immutable record of transactions, making it easier to track shipments, verify authenticity, and prevent fraud. This technology is particularly valuable for industries like pharmaceuticals and high-value goods.

Collaboration and outsourcing in transportation management have become essential strategies for businesses seeking to optimize their supply chains. By working with 3PL providers, suppliers, and customers, companies can achieve cost efficiencies, improve service levels, and enhance operational flexibility. Effective collaboration requires strategic alignment, robust communication, and a commitment to mutual success.

As the logistics landscape continues to evolve, leveraging innovations in technology, sustainability practices, and predictive analytics will enable companies to stay competitive. Building strong, long-term relationships with 3PL partners and other supply chain stakeholders will remain critical for navigating the complexities of transportation management in a globalized economy. By embracing collaboration and innovation, businesses can position themselves for sustainable growth and success in the future.

Chapter 13: Transportation Challenges in Global Trade

Transportation in International Markets

Challenges of Cross-Border and Long-Distance Transportation

Trade Agreements and Global Supply Chain Dynamics

Mitigating Risks in Global Transportation

Global trade relies heavily on efficient and reliable transportation systems to connect markets, facilitate economic growth, and support the movement of goods across borders. However, international transportation comes with unique challenges, including navigating complex regulations, managing risks, and addressing the logistical intricacies of long-distance and cross-border shipments. This chapter explores the key issues facing transportation in global trade and offers strategies for overcoming these challenges.

13.1 Transportation in International Markets

International transportation plays a vital role in global trade by linking producers, distributors, and consumers across continents. It supports diverse industries, from manufacturing and agriculture to retail and technology, enabling the exchange of goods and services on a global scale.

13.1.1 Importance of International Transportation

Facilitating Market Access: International transportation enables companies to access global markets, expand customer bases, and diversify revenue streams.

Supporting Supply Chains: Efficient transportation ensures timely delivery of raw materials and finished products, keeping global supply chains operational.

Driving Economic Growth: Reliable transportation infrastructure contributes to economic development by fostering international trade and investment.

13.1.2 Key Components of International Transportation

Freight Forwarding: Coordinating shipments across multiple modes of transport and managing customs processes.

Port Operations: Ensuring efficient loading and unloading of goods at major sea and air ports.

Global Logistics Networks: Leveraging a combination of road, rail, sea, and air transportation to move goods across countries and continents.

13.2 Challenges of Cross-Border and Long-Distance Transportation

Transporting goods across borders and over long distances introduces unique complexities that can disrupt supply chains and increase costs.

13.2.1 Regulatory and Customs Issues

Complex Documentation: Cross-border shipments require extensive paperwork, including customs declarations, import/export licenses, and certificates of origin.

Regulatory Variability: Different countries have varying trade regulations, product standards, and safety requirements, complicating compliance.

Delays at Borders: Customs clearance processes can cause significant delays, especially in regions with limited infrastructure or stringent inspection protocols.

13.2.2 Infrastructure and Connectivity

Inadequate Infrastructure: In developing regions, poor transportation infrastructure, such as limited road and rail networks, can hinder trade.

Logistical Bottlenecks: Congested ports and inefficient handling of goods can disrupt supply chains and delay deliveries.

Geographical Challenges: Long-distance transportation often involves traversing remote or difficult terrain, adding to the complexity of logistics.

13.2.3 Cultural and Communication Barriers

Language Differences: Miscommunication due to language barriers can lead to errors in documentation and coordination.

Cultural Variations: Understanding local business practices and etiquette is essential for smooth transportation operations.

13.2.4 Security Concerns

Theft and Piracy: High-value shipments are vulnerable to theft during transit, particularly in regions prone to organized crime or piracy.

Fraud and Counterfeit Goods: International trade involves risks related to fraud, counterfeit goods, and unauthorized alterations to shipments.

13.3 Trade Agreements and Global Supply Chain Dynamics

Trade agreements and international regulations significantly influence transportation in global trade, shaping the flow of goods and services across borders.

13.3.1 The Role of Trade Agreements

Facilitating Trade: Agreements like the World Trade Organization (WTO) framework, NAFTA/USMCA, and the

European Union Customs Union simplify trade by reducing tariffs and streamlining customs procedures.

Encouraging Regional Collaboration: Trade blocs such as ASEAN and Mercosur promote economic integration and improve regional transportation networks.

Standardizing Practices: Harmonized trade regulations enhance consistency and predictability in international transportation.

13.3.2 Global Supply Chain Dynamics

Demand Volatility: Fluctuations in global demand can disrupt transportation schedules and strain logistics networks.

Seasonal Variations: Peak shipping seasons, such as the holiday period, increase competition for transportation capacity, driving up costs.

Geopolitical Factors: Political instability, trade wars, and sanctions can affect the availability and reliability of transportation routes.

13.4 Mitigating Risks in Global Transportation

To navigate the challenges of international transportation, businesses must adopt proactive risk management strategies and leverage advanced tools and technologies.

13.4.1 Strategic Planning and Diversification

Diversifying Transport Modes: Using a mix of road, rail, sea, and air transport reduces reliance on a single mode and increases flexibility.

Establishing Alternative Routes: Planning contingency routes minimizes the impact of disruptions caused by natural disasters, geopolitical events, or infrastructure failures.

Supplier and Carrier Diversification: Working with multiple suppliers and carriers reduces dependency on a single source, enhancing resilience.

13.4.2 Technology and Real-Time Visibility

Track and Trace Solutions: GPS and IoT-enabled tracking systems provide real-time updates on shipment locations, improving visibility and control.

Predictive Analytics: Data-driven tools help anticipate potential delays, optimize routes, and forecast demand, ensuring more reliable transportation.

Blockchain for Security: Blockchain technology enhances the security of international shipments by creating an immutable ledger of transactions.

13.4.3 Collaboration and Partnerships

Strong Partner Relationships: Collaborating with reliable logistics providers, customs brokers, and trade consultants ensures smoother operations.

Cross-Border Alliances: Building partnerships with stakeholders in target markets fosters trust and simplifies coordination.

13.4.4 Insurance and Risk Transfer

Comprehensive Coverage: Securing insurance policies tailored to international transportation risks, such as cargo damage, theft, or delay, mitigates financial losses.

Contractual Protections: Using contracts to define roles, responsibilities, and liability limits clarifies expectations and reduces disputes.

13.5 Case Studies on Overcoming Global Transportation Challenges

Case Study 1: Managing Port Congestion

A major electronics manufacturer faced delays due to congestion at a key Asian port. By rerouting shipments to nearby secondary ports and collaborating with local logistics providers, the company reduced delays and maintained supply chain continuity.

Case Study 2: Mitigating Geopolitical Risks

A European apparel retailer diversified its transportation network to avoid routes affected by trade sanctions. By leveraging alternative carriers and sourcing from multiple regions, the retailer minimized disruptions and sustained operations.

Global transportation is a cornerstone of international trade, enabling businesses to connect with markets worldwide. However, navigating the complexities of cross-border logistics requires a deep understanding of regulatory frameworks, geopolitical dynamics, and operational challenges. By adopting strategic risk management practices, leveraging advanced technologies, and building strong partnerships, businesses can overcome these challenges and thrive in the global marketplace. As global trade continues to evolve, staying adaptable and proactive will be key to ensuring seamless and efficient transportation operations.

Chapter 14: Future Trends in Transportation Management

The Impact of Autonomous Vehicles and Drones

Hyperloop and Other Emerging Modes of Transportation

The Shift Towards Digital and Smart Transportation Networks

Adapting to Future Changes in the Transportation Landscape

The transportation industry is undergoing rapid transformation, driven by technological advancements, shifting consumer expectations, and the pressing need for sustainability. The future of transportation management promises unprecedented efficiency, connectivity, and innovation, revolutionizing the movement of goods and services. This chapter explores the most significant trends shaping the future of transportation and their implications for supply chain operations.

14.1 The Impact of Autonomous Vehicles and Drones

Autonomous vehicles and drones are redefining transportation management, offering solutions that enhance speed, efficiency, and safety. These technologies are poised to become integral components of modern logistics.

14.1.1 Autonomous Vehicles

Autonomous trucks and cars equipped with advanced sensors, cameras, and AI algorithms are transforming the transportation landscape.

Benefits:

Enhanced Efficiency: Autonomous vehicles can operate 24/7, reducing delivery times and increasing productivity.

Cost Savings: Lower reliance on human drivers reduces labor costs.

Improved Safety: AI-powered systems minimize human error, reducing accidents.

Challenges:

Regulatory hurdles and public acceptance.

High initial investment in technology and infrastructure.

Ethical concerns regarding decision-making in critical situations.

Applications:

Long-haul freight transportation using autonomous trucks.

Last-mile delivery in urban areas.

14.1.2 Drones in Transportation

Drones are becoming a game-changer, especially for last-mile delivery and accessing remote areas.

Key Applications:

Delivery of small packages in urban and rural settings.

Monitoring infrastructure such as pipelines and railroads.

Disaster relief by delivering essential supplies.

Advantages:

Speed and Accessibility: Drones bypass traffic congestion and reach inaccessible areas.

Cost Efficiency: Reduced need for traditional delivery vehicles.

Eco-Friendliness: Lower carbon emissions compared to conventional methods.

Challenges:

Limited payload capacity.

Airspace regulations and privacy concerns.

Reliability in adverse weather conditions.

14.2 Hyperloop and Other Emerging Modes of Transportation

Emerging transportation technologies like the hyperloop promise to revolutionize the speed and efficiency of moving goods and people.

14.2.1 The Hyperloop

The hyperloop, a high-speed transportation system using magnetic levitation in vacuum-sealed tubes, is a futuristic mode of transport with transformative potential.

Features:

Speeds exceeding 600 miles per hour.

Energy-efficient and eco-friendly operations.

Minimal ground space requirements.

Impact on Supply Chains:

Significant reductions in lead times for long-distance shipments.

Enhanced connectivity between major trade hubs.

Increased viability of just-in-time (JIT) inventory systems.

14.2.2 Other Emerging Technologies

Electric Vertical Take-Off and Landing (eVTOL) Vehicles:

Ideal for urban transportation and short-distance freight delivery.

Reduces traffic congestion and dependence on ground transportation.

Magnetic Levitation (Maglev) Trains:

Ultra-fast trains with minimal friction, offering efficient long-distance transport solutions.

14.3 The Shift Towards Digital and Smart Transportation Networks

Digitalization is reshaping transportation management by enabling greater connectivity, real-time visibility, and data-driven decision-making.

14.3.1 Internet of Things (IoT) and Connected Systems

IoT-enabled sensors and devices provide real-time monitoring of vehicles, cargo, and infrastructure.

Applications:

Tracking shipment locations and conditions (temperature, humidity, etc.).

Predictive maintenance of vehicles to reduce downtime.

Dynamic route optimization based on traffic and weather conditions.

14.3.2 Artificial Intelligence (AI) and Machine Learning

AI-driven tools are optimizing transportation management in various ways:

Demand Forecasting: Accurate prediction of transportation needs based on historical data and market trends.

Dynamic Pricing Models: AI algorithms adjust pricing based on demand, fuel costs, and capacity.

Autonomous Decision-Making: AI systems recommend optimal routes, carriers, and modes.

14.3.3 Blockchain Technology

Blockchain ensures secure and transparent transactions in transportation management.

Benefits:

Enhanced traceability of goods across the supply chain.

Reduction in fraud and counterfeit goods.

Streamlined documentation for cross-border transportation.

14.3.4 Digital Twins

Digital twins create virtual models of transportation networks to simulate and optimize operations.

Applications:

Testing the impact of new routes and schedules.

Predicting the effects of disruptions on supply chain performance.

14.4 Adapting to Future Changes in the Transportation Landscape

The transportation industry must remain agile to adapt to rapid changes, including technological advancements, regulatory shifts, and evolving consumer demands.

14.4.1 Embracing Sustainability

As sustainability becomes a core focus, transportation management will increasingly prioritize eco-friendly practices.

Carbon Neutral Initiatives:

Adoption of electric and hydrogen-powered vehicles.

Development of carbon offset programs for freight transportation.

Circular Logistics:

Designing transportation networks to support recycling and reuse of materials.

14.4.2 Enhancing Collaboration

Collaboration across the supply chain will be critical to navigating future challenges.

Shared Transportation Networks:

Companies pooling resources for cost-effective and efficient freight transportation.

Enhanced collaboration between competitors to reduce empty miles.

Global Standardization:

Harmonizing transportation regulations and standards for seamless international trade.

14.4.3 Workforce Transformation

As automation becomes more prevalent, the workforce will require reskilling to adapt to new roles.

Upskilling Initiatives:

Training employees to operate and maintain advanced technologies.

Emphasizing data analytics and technology management skills.

Focus on Human-Machine Collaboration:

Leveraging human creativity alongside AI and robotics for optimal decision-making.

14.5 Conclusion

The future of transportation management is marked by groundbreaking technological advancements and a growing emphasis on sustainability. Autonomous vehicles, drones, and emerging technologies like hyperloop and digital twins are transforming the way goods and services are transported. At the same time, digitalization and smart networks are enabling unparalleled efficiency and transparency.

To remain competitive in this evolving landscape, businesses must embrace innovation, foster collaboration, and proactively adapt to emerging trends. By doing so, they can create resilient, efficient, and sustainable transportation systems that meet the demands of a rapidly changing world. The journey ahead is one of transformation, offering limitless opportunities for those ready to embrace the future of transportation management.

Chapter 15: Conclusion and Best Practices for Effective Transportation Management

Recap of Key Strategies and Best Practices

Integrating Transportation Management with Overall Business Goals

Building a Resilient and Adaptable Transportation System

Final Thoughts on the Future of Transportation Management

Transportation management is the backbone of modern supply chain operations, facilitating the seamless movement of goods and services from origin to destination. As we conclude our exploration of this dynamic field, it is crucial to summarize the key strategies, highlight best practices, and emphasize the integration of transportation management into broader business goals. This chapter also envisions a resilient, adaptable future for transportation systems.

15.1 Recap of Key Strategies and Best Practices

Over the course of this book, we have examined various aspects of transportation management. Below, we summarize the essential strategies and practices that can drive effectiveness and efficiency:

15.1.1 Route Planning and Optimization

Leverage advanced tools like Transportation Management Systems (TMS) to design optimal routes.

Incorporate real-time data from GPS and IoT sensors to adjust for traffic, weather, or disruptions.

Prioritize cost and lead-time minimization while maintaining service quality.

15.1.2 Modal Selection

Evaluate the characteristics of different transportation modes (road, rail, air, sea, pipeline) based on speed, cost, and cargo requirements.

Balance short-term cost savings with long-term sustainability considerations.

Apply multi-modal strategies for flexibility and efficiency.

15.1.3 Fleet Management

Maintain a well-structured fleet maintenance schedule to reduce downtime and prolong asset life.

Incorporate fuel-efficient vehicles and explore innovative options like electric and autonomous fleets.

Monitor fleet performance using digital dashboards to ensure optimal utilization.

15.1.4 Risk Mitigation

Identify and assess risks, including delays, accidents, theft, and environmental challenges.

Develop contingency plans and establish strong relationships with insurance providers.

Use technology like blockchain to enhance security and transparency in transportation processes.

15.1.5 Sustainability Initiatives

Implement green transportation practices, such as route optimization, load consolidation, and eco-friendly vehicles.

Set measurable goals for reducing carbon emissions and energy consumption.

Collaborate with stakeholders to develop circular logistics systems and reduce environmental impact.

15.1.6 Technology Integration

Adopt TMS, AI, IoT, and blockchain technologies to streamline operations and improve decision-making.

Use predictive analytics for demand forecasting and proactive risk management.

Stay ahead by exploring future trends, such as autonomous vehicles, drones, and hyperloop systems.

15.2 Integrating Transportation Management with Overall Business Goals

Transportation management does not operate in isolation; it is a strategic function that aligns closely with organizational objectives. Effective integration requires a holistic approach:

15.2.1 Aligning with Strategic Goals

Support organizational priorities like cost leadership, differentiation, or sustainability through tailored transportation strategies.

Collaborate with cross-functional teams to ensure that transportation aligns with procurement, production, and customer service.

15.2.2 Enhancing Customer Satisfaction

Use transportation as a key differentiator by ensuring timely and reliable deliveries.

Offer flexible delivery options, including expedited shipping and last-mile tracking.

Monitor customer feedback to continuously refine transportation processes.

15.2.3 Cost Management and Efficiency

Optimize transportation budgets without compromising service quality.

Invest in technology and innovation to achieve long-term cost savings.

Regularly review transportation costs against industry benchmarks and adjust strategies accordingly.

15.3 Building a Resilient and Adaptable Transportation System

Resilience and adaptability are essential for navigating the uncertainties and disruptions inherent in transportation management. Organizations can prepare for future challenges by:

15.3.1 Developing Contingency Plans

Create robust risk management frameworks that address various scenarios, including natural disasters, geopolitical conflicts, and supply chain bottlenecks.

Maintain buffer inventory and alternate transportation routes for critical shipments.

15.3.2 Leveraging Collaboration

Foster strong partnerships with suppliers, customers, and third-party logistics (3PL) providers.

Share information and resources to build a more integrated and responsive transportation network.

Engage in collaborative risk mitigation initiatives, such as shared warehousing and pooled distribution.

15.3.3 Embracing Innovation

Stay informed about technological advancements and incorporate relevant innovations into your operations.

Encourage a culture of continuous improvement to remain competitive in an ever-changing landscape.

Pilot new technologies, such as autonomous vehicles or AI-driven optimization tools, to evaluate their impact on efficiency and performance.

15.4 Final Thoughts on the Future of Transportation Management

The field of transportation management is poised for an exciting future, characterized by rapid technological advancements, increasing globalization, and growing emphasis on sustainability. As businesses adapt to these changes, they must remain proactive, resilient, and customer-focused.

Embracing Change: Companies that prioritize innovation, digitalization, and collaboration will be better positioned to thrive in a competitive environment.

Sustainability as a Priority: Organizations must integrate green initiatives into their transportation strategies to meet regulatory demands and societal expectations.

Customer-Centric Focus: As consumers demand faster, more reliable deliveries, transportation management must evolve to meet these expectations without sacrificing efficiency.

Transportation management is more than a logistical function; it is a strategic enabler of business success. By implementing best practices, leveraging technology, and aligning operations with broader goals, organizations can build robust transportation systems that drive value, foster resilience, and contribute to a sustainable future.

"Transportation is the lifeline of global commerce, connecting people, goods, and ideas across the world. Effective transportation management is not just about moving cargo; it's about driving efficiency, innovation, and sustainability. Let this book inspire you to master the art of seamless logistics, adapt to evolving challenges, and pave the way for a smarter, greener, and more connected future in transportation."

www.ingramcontent.com/pod-product-compliance
Lightning Source LLC
Chambersburg PA
CBHW071508220526
45472CB00003B/952